INFRASTRUCTURE
FOR ALL

INFRASTRUCTURE FOR ALL

Meeting the needs of both men and women in development projects
— A practical guide for engineers, technicians and project managers —

Water, Engineering and Development Centre
Loughborough University
2007

WEDC

Water, Engineering and Development Centre
Loughborough University
Leicestershire
LE11 3TU UK

t: +44 (0) 1509 222885
f: +44 (0) 1509 211079
e: wedc@lboro.ac.uk
http://www.lboro.ac.uk/wedc/

© WEDC, Loughborough University, 2007

Reed, B.J., Coates, S. and Parry-Jones, S. et al. (2007)
Infrastructure for All: Meeting the needs of both men and women in development projects – a practical guide for engineers, technicians and project managers

WEDC, Loughborough University, UK.

ISBN Paperback 978 1 84380 109 2
ISBN Library Ebook: 978 1 78853 306 5
Book DOI: http://dx.doi.org/10.3362/9781788533065

A catalogue record for this book is available from the British Library.

This edition is reprinted and distributed by Practical Action Publishing.

Since 1974, Practical Action Publishing has published and disseminated books and information in support of international development work throughout the world. Practical Action Publishing trades only in support of its parent charity objectives and any profits are covenanted back to Practical Action (Charity Reg. No. 247257, Group VAT Registration No. 880 9924 76).

Designed, illustrated and produced by
Rod Shaw, Kay Davey and Ken Chatterton

Find out more about WEDC Publications online at:
http://www.lboro.ac.uk/wedc/publications/

Acknowledgements

These guidelines were produced by a project team consisting of Sue Coates, Marie Fry, Sarah Parry-Jones and Brian Reed, led by Ian Smout, with editorial contributions by Brian Appleton. The team wishes to thank the following people for their assistance in preparing this publication.

The project was advised by an international review group, consisting of: Alison Barrett, Morag Bell, Lizette Burgers, John Collett, Brendan A Doyle, Louiza Duncker, Ben Fawcett, Martin Gillham, Sarah House, Jeremy Ockelford, Archana Patkar, Peter Sinclair, Rupert Talbot, and Renu Gera and Ilse Wilson

These people reviewed drafts of the guidelines and the final draft was also peer reviewed in detail by the UK Department for International Development (DFID). Special mention is made of the contribution of Sarah House in laying the foundations for this project. Thanks must also go to the students and staff members of WEDC and Loughborough University who contributed material and comments for the project, especially: Paul Deverill, Julie Fisher, Margaret Ince, Hazel Jones, Rose Lidonde, Cyrus Njiru, Rebecca Scott, Brian Skinner, and Mike Smith.

The research and development of this book and the associated training material were assisted by the following partner organisations: Mvula Trust (South Africa), CSIR (South Africa) and UNICEF (India), together with the valuable contributions by staff from UNICEF (Nigeria), WaterAid (Zambia), and Médecins sans Frontières (International). Case studies were obtained from a wide variety of contributors.

The funding for the project was provided by DFID as part of its Knowledge and Research programme for the benefit of developing countries. This book is one of the outputs from project R7129. The views expressed are not necessarily those of DFID.

How to use this guide

This guide is for engineers, technicians and project managers who want to ensure that the infrastructure and services they provide are suitable for the whole of society. Part of this process is having an awareness of gender issues. Matching engineering practice to the needs of the community requires engineers to understand how society works and how to find out what people require from engineering projects. This means men and women have to be involved in all stages of the project.

Much of the knowledge and skills required has not been included in engineering education and training courses in the past. The first four chapters of this guide give an overview of some of the community issues that engineers need to be aware of throughout the project cycle and what links these to the engineer's role. They should be read through to provide the necessary background for the later chapters, although they do not aim to cover issues such as participation, poverty or gender in detail. Other publications and professionals can provide guidance in these areas. Even if the reader is familiar with the social issues, these chapters should be of interest, because they have been written around engineering issues, rather than the socio-economic or rights-based frameworks that much of the literature in this subject is based on. The guide also has a practical focus which will be useful for gender specialists with little field experience.

The later chapters move from the why? and what? to the more detailed question: how? They give specific, practical examples of how engineers can involve men and women in development projects in order to match infrastructure with their needs. These chapters can be used as a source book for inspiration and guidance on appropriate designs and construction techniques.

For training material to complement this book, see Reed, B.J. and Coates S. *Developing Engineers and Technicians – Notes on giving guidance to engineers and technicians on how infrastructure can meet the needs of men and women.* WEDC, Loughborough University, 2007

Evidence for placing the needs of men and women at the centre of infrastructure development is provided in figures, case studies and comments in boxes used throughout the book, illustrating ways of involving men and women in engineering projects. More empirical evidence is given is a series of statistical analyses of why projects succeed or fail.

Preface

Engineers have recognised that rich and poor communities are different socially, culturally, economically and physically. Providing a single standard of infrastructure for every situation does not work. Appropriate technologies have been developed to provide sustainable services for communities with limited resources. Handpumps, pit latrines and small-scale irrigation may provide a better service over time than water treatment works, piped sewerage or large irrigation canals.

Men and women are also different socially, culturally, economically and physically. Social scientists address these gender differences, but there is a recognition that this should not be dealt with in isolation. These guidelines have been developed to demonstrate how engineers can provide infrastructure such as water supplies, sanitation, irrigation and transport that is appropriate for everybody. This includes the full range of technology from conventional large-scale systems to lower cost, local solutions.

This is not a 'gender' book. The research that resulted in these guidelines showed that there is a gap between standard gender textbooks and standard engineering textbooks. This book aims to fill the gap from a technical perspective. Discussions with engineers showed that what was required was information on how technical staff can ensure that their product is suitable for both men and women. This was requested in a format and language that related to engineering, rather than social issues. This perspective may also be useful for social personnel working with or training engineers.

Gender books tend to concentrate on rights and policies. Engineers are more product focused. These guidelines introduce ways to translate those policies into practical outcomes, through adjusting the engineering process so that the design criteria for infrastructure address the demands of all users.

Just as the engineering process and product alter when gender issues are taken into account, the gender process and product will alter to fit the engineering context. The focus, timescale and resources of most infrastructure development projects can readily address the practical needs of socially excluded groups, but there are fewer opportunities within these projects to provide the longer-term strategic actions that should accompany such developments. Whilst a superficial review of these guidelines may suggest a welfare or women in development approach, the research has shown that the longer-term strategic gender issues need to be addressed from a team perspective. Engineers can provide those essential inputs that social scientists cannot provide. Water, sanitation and the local development of infrastructure are good entry points to community development, but other professionals need to build on the foundations the engineering profession lays down.

One of the communication barriers between engineers, social scientists and the communities they are working with is the use of specialist language. This can mean people do not understand or even misinterpret what one group is saying. Every branch of engineering has its own specialised vocabulary that can make it difficult for non-engineers to understand, for example 'sewage', 'sewers' and 'sewerage'. Social scientists also use specific terms to describe social factors such as 'sex' and 'gender'. This book tries to limit the use of jargon, but some terms have to be used, as they describe precise concepts. Understanding these concepts will make socio-economic issues clearer. Where possible, explanations are given in footnotes.

Throughout this publication, vulnerable groups are highlighted as needing special attention if their infrastructure needs are not to be ignored. Various terms are used such as 'socially excluded', 'socially disadvantaged', 'vulnerable' or more specifically, 'the poor', women, disabled, children, the old, low caste or class, refugees or religious or ethnic minorities. Whilst gender and economic status are significant indicators of social disadvantage, the pattern of social exclusion will vary from place to place and this should be considered whilst reading this book.

Foreword

This valuable book aims to help civil engineers ensure that the facilities they design and build are beneficial to all members of society. Using lots of examples, especially examples related to water and sanitation, the book demonstrates that one size does not fit all. It shows how women, men and children frequently have different needs and different priorities. They use infrastructure in different ways. They are socially positioned in different ways, and have differing amounts of power. It explains how the 'community' that will use the infrastructure is generally structured by inequalities of various kinds. The engineer may intend that the facility should serve the needs of all; but if there is no analysis of social, and well as geological, stratification, then this intention is not likely to be realized.

The book seeks to make gender analysis intelligible to engineers working at the project level; to equip them to co-operate with social scientists, and to sensitize them to the need to work with women and men in the user community. Gender is presented as a form of social stratification that intersects with other forms of stratification, such as class, caste, and ethnicity. The emphasis is on the practical ways in which taking account of gender relations will improve the design, implementation and use of infrastructure.

With this in mind, the book sensibly does not enter into the finer points of debates among specialist gender analysts. It concentrates on what engineers need to know to improve their projects, to give the 'civil' aspects of their work equal weight with the 'engineering' aspects. An important aspect of the approach adopted is to present gender relations as capable of change, not as set in stone.

For instance, collecting water is currently seen as a job for girls and women in many rural areas. As a case study from Zambia explains 'It was not seemly for men to carry buckets on their head or wade into muddy water.' But this division of labour began to change when plastic jerry cans were introduced to collect water – they could be carried on bicycles or carts; and when improvements at the water sources removed the need for wading in water. Men began to do more of the work of collecting water. Some of women's time was freed for other activities: an important gain in societies in which women tend to have longer working hours than men, a gain that addresses both women's practical, everyday, here-and-now needs; and their longer run, strategic needs for more say in how their societies are run. If women have to spend less time fetching water, they have the possibility of time free to attend meetings where key decisions are taken, a necessary, if not a sufficient step, towards infrastructure for all.

Professor Diane Elson,
Department of Sociology,
University of Essex

Contents

Figures

1

What (or who) is infrastructure for?

The role of a civil engineer is to serve society. Engineers fulfil that role by developing infrastructure projects — roads, bridges, dams, canals, water supply systems, sewers, drains, railways, power systems, communication systems and buildings. Most infrastructure projects have both positive and negative impacts: economic, social and environmental. The challenge is to produce net benefits for all sections of society, including the marginalized groups whose voices are not readily heard in the corridors of power.

In this chapter, we look at the varying needs of different groups in society and the potential pitfalls of a 'one solution fits all' approach to infrastructure development. The implication for engineers is that they must recognize and take account of a wide range of societal parameters alongside their more familiar technical analyses. The key points discussed in this chapter are:

- Infrastructure is not a neutral issue. *What* is built has different impacts on men and women, rich and poor, young and old, able-bodied and disabled, and other divisions in society.

- *How* infrastructure is provided can have a positive impact on society, providing opportunities for men and women — commercially, personally, as a community and in the household.

- To develop appropriate infrastructure for all, engineers need to appreciate the diversity of society and the different opportunities open to people to express their views and influence decisions.

- Differences between men and women are both physical (sexual) and social (gender), and societies are also divided by disability, class, religion, tribe or caste — all of which may have a bearing on the choice of technologies and service levels that are suitable.

What is infrastructure?

The permanent, public, physical services that society constructs include roads, bridges, dams, water supply systems, canals, sewers, drains, railways, power systems, communication systems and buildings. These are produced for a variety of reasons:

- to support economic activity;
- to protect or enhance the environment;
- to improve living conditions; or
- as political gestures.

A bridge is not built just to cross a river; an irrigation canal is not built just to provide water. Infrastructure has an economic, environmental or social purpose.

The uses of infrastructure

Infrastructure serves the needs of society, but as no society is totally equal, the use of infrastructure is not a neutral issue. Men and women, rich and poor, able-bodied and disabled, high and low social status people will all use infrastructure in different ways because their work, resources and opportunities vary. Work may be *commercial, domestic, community* or *personal*. Evaluating the potential impacts and working with local men and women to develop appropriate solutions should be just as much a part of normal practice for engineers as building safety and durability into their designs. The following introduction provides some examples of the impact of the development of infrastructure on men and women. It illustrates the type of issues that engineers may need to take into account when framing infrastructure projects.

A bridge too far

"A road was planned to be upgraded to improve the transport links to a remote town. However, this would open up an area of forest to illegal logging, with all the environmental and social impact that this would have on the local people. A compromise suggested in the environmental impact study was to omit upgrading of the bridges on the road. This would enable the small vans used for local transport to operate freely, but restrict the use of large trucks, rendering large-scale deforestation uneconomic."

J. Purseglove, Personal communication

Transport facilities

Transport facilities do not just enhance large and small-scale *commercial* activities, but can bring additional services to a settlement. Mobile banking and visiting medical services are facilitated by easy access and can benefit women who have less opportunity to travel, thus making *domestic* activities easier. Improved transport can also reduce the price of goods, to the benefit of the household budget. Access to cheaper fuel reduces the burden of women collecting firewood. Good transport links can reduce the price of food and make its supply more secure. Good communication links can enhance *community* activities by making it easier for men and women to attend meetings and vote in elections. Reducing travel times allows women to attend markets, have a job or carry out public service alongside their domestic activities. A route that optimises long-distance travel may bypass small towns, reducing opportunities for poor men and women to benefit from passing trade and to have access to transport.

Figure 1.1 shows how main roads are just part of a larger transport system that connects people.

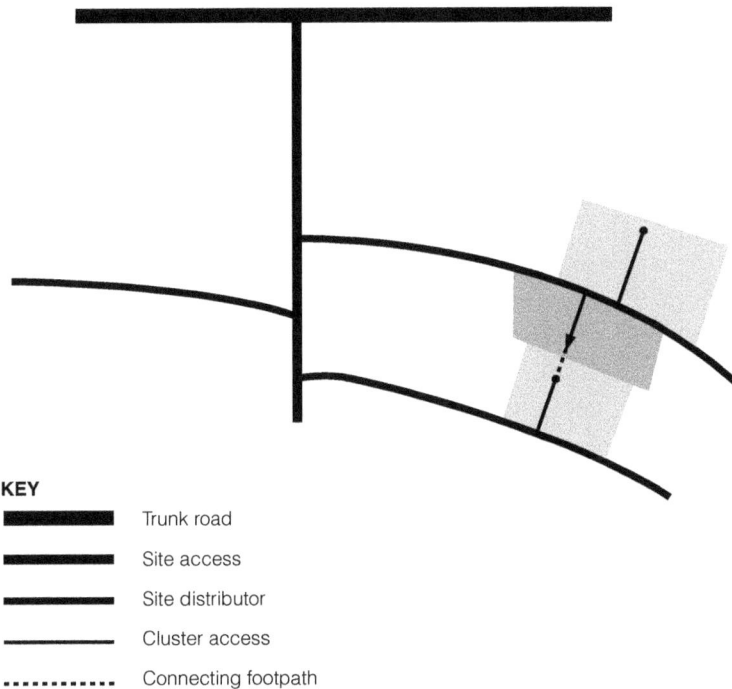

KEY

━━━━━━━ Trunk road

━━━━━━━ Site access

━━━━━━━ Site distributor

───── Cluster access

············ Connecting footpath

Figure 1.1. A hierarchy of access routes

Roads make a difference

An Oxfam project had problems in reaching 90% of villages in the West of Sudan, the only access being by foot or donkey. After the construction of 85km of roads, the time and distance required to undertake basic tasks, such as collect water or visit the health centre dropped.

Barday village

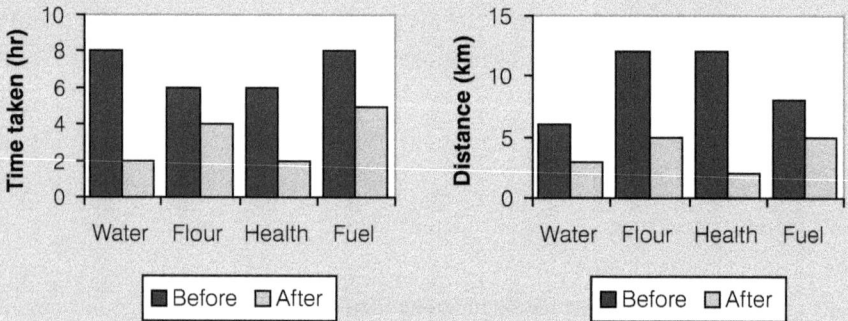

Note that time is often more significant than distance in increasing access.

'Feeder Roads and Food Security' by Suad Mustafa Elhaj Musa in *Balancing the load: Women, gender and transport,* eds. P Fernando and G Porter (2002), Zed Books/IFRTD London

Drive carefully

"After clinical depression, road traffic accidents are the second biggest cause of loss of 'active' life due to illness and death for men in developing regions. This is measured in the number of years lost through disability or death (Disability Adjusted Life Years — DALYs) in 1990 (pre-HIV/AIDS). Road accidents do not feature in the top ten causes of disease or injury for women in developing regions, but are the second and third causes for men and women respectively in developed regions."

Engendering Development — Through Gender Equality in Rights, Resources and Voice (2001), World Bank Policy Research Report

Good road design also has a *personal* dimension. Road improvements that increase the speed of trucks and buses can lead to an increase in road casualties. Women and children are more likely to be walking, so attention to pedestrian needs can reduce risks from road accidents or violence to these groups.

Agricultural support

In some countries there is a clear divide between male-dominated *commercial* agriculture and the more fragmented, poor and female-dominated *domestic* sector. Irrigation schemes can inadvertently have a male bias, as they provide water to the defined landholdings of commercial farmers, rather than to the poor with insecure land tenure, growing produce on a smaller scale. On the other hand, irrigation generally increases job opportunities for the landless poor, especially women, who often have traditional roles in weeding. The extended growing season provides work when there is none to do on non-irrigated land. Increased food security, extended cropping seasons and lower food prices through irrigation can benefit the whole family.

Where produce is grown at home, infrastructure can be adapted to meet domestic requirements. Watering may be carried out using a bucket or watering can, so a water point provided near the smallholding can reduce the burden of carrying water and thus increase the production of crops. Irrigation can also be integrated with other infrastructure developments, such as using road drainage, wastewater from treatment works or spillage from handpumps to water gardens or wood lots. These can provide a *community* irrigation facility.

Why people get schistosomiasis

Gender and age-specific analysis of reported data for urinary schistosomiasis (bilharzia) in a project area showed that this water-related disease was most common amongst schoolboys and girls/women between 10 and 40 years of age. The incidence among boys was related to the boys' swimming habits; while for women and girls the disease was associated with the local practice of washing clothes while standing in bilharzia-infested water.

This finding had implications both for the hygiene education programme and for a wells project, which had banned washing clothes at the handpumps and so forced women to continue their use of open water.

Irrigation water is not just used for agriculture. Water can be collected for domestic use or used for *personal* activities, such as washing or swimming. Irrigation developments need to consider the implications of these uses, to avoid any problems from vector-borne diseases, such as malaria or schistosomiasis.[1]

Water, sanitation and hygiene [2,3]

Water is a vital resource for both large and small-scale commercial activities and access to water can directly stimulate the economy. It is especially important for industries based on women's traditional roles such as food preparation, laundry and healthcare. Large industries can manage their own water supplies, but small-scale enterprises depend on public systems. Waste disposal from large and small industries will have an impact on the environment, but the poor will suffer more, due to their reduced options about where they live, where they grow their food and where they get their water.

Women's role in managing domestic water supplies is one of the clearest areas of infrastructure having a gender impact. The time and effort taken to collect water and the disease caused by inadequate water and sanitation are well documented and the burden of both these impacts falls largely on women. Water is used for drinking, cooking, cleaning and washing.

Improved sanitation and hygiene practices impact particularly on women, through reduced illness in the family and personal benefits. Culturally appropriate latrines that are easy to clean improve both personal and domestic activities.

Often lack of access to water and sanitation services is due to the low priority it is given by the community, as the richer male leaders do not directly experience the problems associated with a lack of adequate water supplies. To give this issue its proper priority, women need to be given a voice in decision-making.

Who is infrastructure for?

It is clear that infrastructure planning and design can affect different people in different ways. What are the implications for a civil engineer instructed

---

1. *Malaria* is spread by mosquitoes that breed in clean water. A trematode worm that spends part of its life cycle in aquatic snails causes *schistosomiasis.*
2. *Environmental sanitation* includes disposal of wastewater, faeces, stormwater, solid waste etc. It is sometimes shortened to sanitation although this can also refer to the safe disposal of faeces only.
3. *Hygiene* includes the use of water and sanitation facilities to reduce disease, for example through hand washing with soap.

A survey of four communities shows a consistent pattern in who collects water, with the chore usually being carried out by women and, to a lesser extent, girls. Improving the water supply infrastructure will therefore benefit these groups of people in particular.

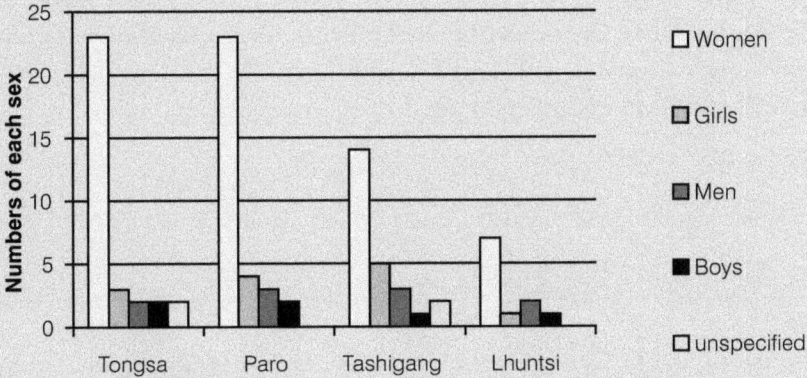

Marie Fry, from data collected in a participatory assessment in Bhutan

by a client to develop an engineering design for specific infrastructure improvements?

The term *civil* in the title civil engineer comes from the Latin word *civis* — a citizen. The work of the civil engineer is bound up with the needs of the people in the society they live in. An early definition of civil engineering was:

> *"The art of directing the great sources of power in Nature for the use and convenience of man."*

Thomas Tredgold, 1788 – 1829

Subsequent definitions may be more technical and less poetic, but an important thread is the notion that the structures and services that a civil engineer produces are for society. Engineers excel at *"directing the great sources of power in Nature"* but perhaps have given the second half of the definition — *"for the use and convenience of man"* less prominence.

In the nineteenth century, the word *man* was used where today we may use *mankind* or *society*. If civil engineers are to provide the infrastructure and services for the use and convenience of society, they need to understand, rather than assume, what society requires of them.

What is society?

Sociologists study society, as geologists study the earth. They categorize people into different groups — by sex, by race, by culture, by social status — as well as considering them as individuals. Geologists do the same, categorizing rocks into groups — sedimentary, igneous, granites, sandstones, as well as understanding that each individual rock will have its own unique chemical composition and strength. Engineers would always recommend a site investigation to find out what the rock is like locally. Should they consider a detailed survey into the local society necessary before starting an engineering project?

Infrastructure improves our environment

Adequate infrastructure is needed by the whole community for roads, drainage and solid waste disposal. Its value is often only appreciated when it is missing.

The two Venn diagrams below are of society and geological rock type. They show the similar processes that professionals use to put some order to the world in which we live. As a subject is investigated, patterns develop that allow us to describe complex systems.

A Venn diagram is a mathematical tool that shows how categories relate to each other. Social scientists use a very similar technique in discussions with communities – but they call them Chapatti diagrams.

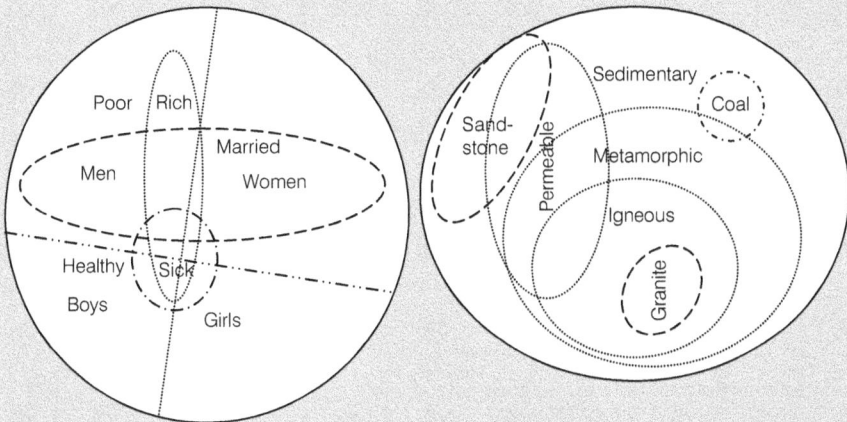

Some categories may be mutually exclusive (male or female – cannot be both); others may be sub-sets of a larger category (boys are a sub-set of male); yet more may overlap (the poor includes men and women)

Different structures are required for different purposes, so a hydrologist needs to know if a rock is permeable or not, whilst someone looking for coal is more interested if the rock is sedimentary.

Society is made up of individuals, but we recognise that coherent groups of people do have similar needs and perspectives. A difficulty is determining what is a personal preference and what is a more widely held concern. Tasks like this require specialist knowledge and skills to identify and assess the true 'demands' of society — just as a geotechnical engineer is called on to carry out site investigations.

Societies are very complicated and a designer cannot be expected to consider the needs of every individual. However, some simplifications can be made. In design, engineers take appropriate worst-case scenarios for key design parameters. These may be adverse structural loading conditions, return periods of floods or strength of materials. These scenarios depend on the risks involved — so a 5 year return period[4] or a flow rate may be suitable for the design of a road drain, but a 10,000 year return period may be more suitable for a dam. These parameters must be relevant and easy to quantify. A similar approach allows social parameters to be covered by worst-case scenarios.

Powerful and weak

The various social groups have different characteristics and these are both physical and social. As not everybody is the same, some groups have advantages over others. Physical strength is an obvious example, with men being stronger than women or children. Some groups have a higher social status than others and there are usually political, legal, religious, economic and cultural variations in a given community. The groups vary between societies and the scale of differences also changes. The less advantaged groups are referred to as *socially excluded, discriminated, vulnerable* or *marginalized*. They have less access to political power, economic opportunities and other aspects such as education or legal protection. These disparities reinforce each other — lack of education leads to fewer economic opportunities; low economic status leads to poorer health; low social status reduces political influence.

A cost benefit analysis[5] of an infrastructure project recognises that there will be both positive and negative impacts. However, a simple cost benefit analysis does not always recognise that the group of people who pay the costs may not be the same as the ones who benefit. Mechanized pumped water may provide increased agricultural output through improved irrigation, but the costs of the lowered groundwater table are borne by those still dependent on handpumps, not by the rich farmers reaping the benefits of irrigation.

Barriers to using infrastructure

Some groups of people can be excluded from decision-making or denied access to public resources and services for a variety of reasons. Typical barriers could be:

---

4. An indication of the probability of a flood of a certain size. For example a flow rate of 10m³/s or more may occur on average every 5 years.
5. Cost benefit analysis aims to find out the total cost of a project over its whole life and compare this to the total benefits that the project will bring.

- social (cultural, religious, legal);
- financial (lack of money, lower wages, no access to credit);
- human (lower educational levels, different health status); and
- physical environment (infrastructure designed for one group only).

"Barriers to infrastructure may combine. An individual impairment (e.g. blindness or having difficulty walking) may prevent a person from accessing education due to the distance and difficulty of travelling to school, the steps up to the classroom, the lack of suitable teaching materials (such as Braille books) and thus the difficulties caused by the initial impairment are compounded by a lack of education.

A person with impairment may be disabled by socio-economic factors. For example, learning difficulties may not be a problem in a rural area where physical labour is common, but may be a problem in a city where it would restrict work that requires reading and writing skills. Conversely, a physical impairment restricting mobility would disable somebody more in a rural area where there are unmade, steep muddy paths, than in an urban setting, where the transport options enable wider employment opportunities.

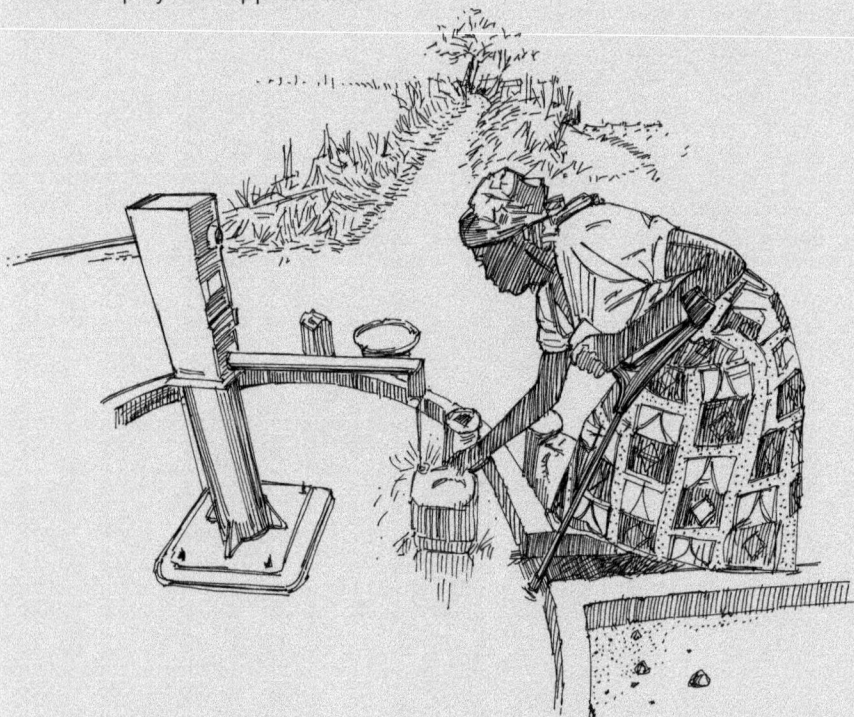

Disability may arise more from society's culture and attitude than from the individual impairment. Albinism (loss of pigment in the skin, eyes and hair) results in visual impairment and skin that is easily sunburnt. Wearing glasses can correct the eyesight, but in many African countries, the individuals are seen as 'ghosts', shunned and refused education and jobs."

Hazel Jones, WEDC

Engineers may consider that their work is neutral — it does not matter if men or women, rich or poor use the infrastructure or service, their needs are the same. This may be true for some technical issues, such as strength of concrete, but is obviously not true for some of the biological differences. Men's physical and social needs have to be considered when designing urinals and women's physical and social needs have to be considered when deciding how to dispose of sanitary towel waste. Neither is it true for social differences. An often-quoted example is the burden of collecting water, which is predominantly a poor woman's role in many countries. There are other areas in water resources, sanitation, irrigation, energy, construction and transport, all of which impact differently on the lives of men and women and all of which can be addressed by engineers.

In terms of meeting the needs of society through the development of infrastructure, the less powerful groups will have a weaker voice in decision-making and less access to the completed product, as they have less money, education or social status. Socially excluded people may be members of distinct cultural, tribal, class or religious groups, but two common indicators are wealth and gender. In most societies, the poor and women will have a lower social status than the rich and men. If the infrastructure is produced so that the most disadvantaged can use it, then it should also be accessible to the rest of society who have fewer obstacles to overcome. However, if the resulting service level is minimal, some will be unwilling to pay to use it. Often there needs to be a range of technology options available to suit different user groups (e.g. handpumps, standposts, house connections).

Choosing public toilets

Users of public toilets in the UK (who are mainly women) wanted:

- more toilets;
- greater accessibility;
- wider cubicles;
- attendants;
- baby changing facilities;
- disabled access; and
- longer opening hours.

Providers (especially local authorities) were concerned with what happens in the 'Gents'. Problems with drug taking, sex and vandalism leads them to discourage use, with limited opening hours, barrier payment systems, narrowing cubicles and surveillance cameras.

Based on Clara Greed in *The Times Higher Education Supplement* (26/7/02)

Men and women, boys and girls

Some of the groups that society is divided into are physically obvious, such as men and women, young and old, able-bodied and disabled. Other groups are less obvious, as the determining factors are socio-economic[6] rather than physical, such as class, caste, wealth or religion. Differences between men and women also fall into this category. Whilst some of the variations between men and women are biological (women menstruate, men are often taller), others are defined by society (men are the breadwinners, women are the homemakers). These latter differences vary between societies and can change over time. To distinguish these social differences between men and women from the biological differences, sociologists use the term 'gender' rather than sex.

Children also need to be considered separately at times — both in terms of addressing their own issues (such as school sanitation) but also as a means of ensuring good practice now and in the future.

Men's work and women's work

Assessing employment

Research has shown that women on the whole work longer hours than men. Reducing their burden by making water collection easier, for example, does not necessarily free time for other income-generating activities but it does redress some of the imbalance between men and women's workloads, reduces the burden on society and improves health. Figure 1.2 shows the imbalance in workloads between men and women.[7]

---

6. *Socio-economic* – social, cultural, economic and financial issues.
7. Example from *Planning for construction and rehabilitation*, PCU/CMMU/WASHE, Zambia.

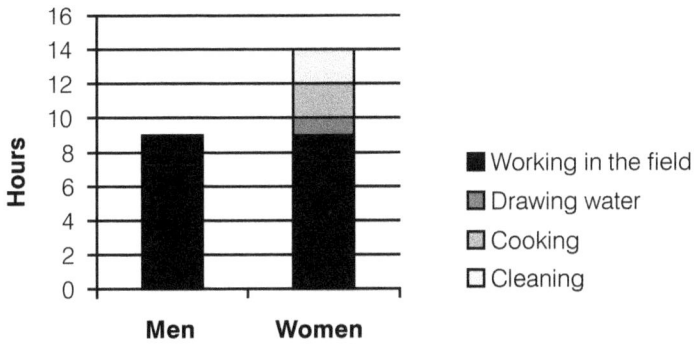

Figure 1.2. Daily hours of labour

An analysis of this kind depends on how you define 'work'. An engineer who is not aware of social disparities may make assumptions and overlook important information. Just as geologists have special methods of assessing the geological situation, social scientists have developed their own set of tools to evaluate the social situation. The clock face diagram (Figure 1.3) is more useful than a bar chart — not only is it easier for people to fill in and understand, but all activities are recorded, without defining if they are 'work' or not.

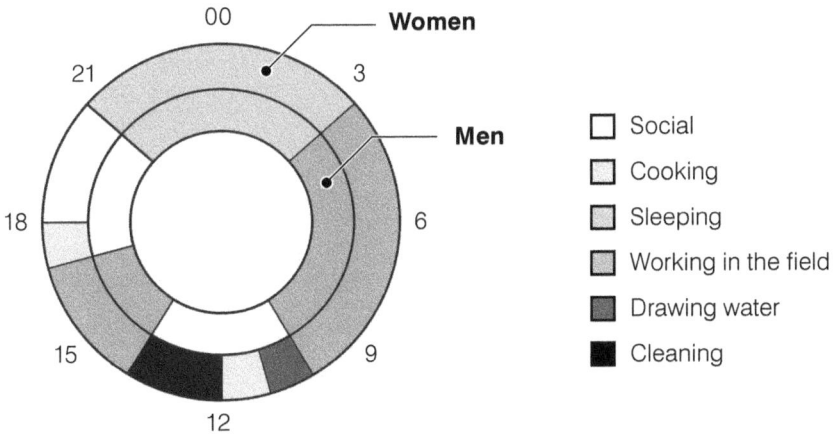

Figure 1.3. Activity profile

This chart could also be used to show when men and women defecate; in some low-income countries, women have to wait until after dark before they can relieve themselves — an additional burden on top of all their other work.

Defining tasks

Work can be categorized as *productive, domestic, community* and *personal*. Women will normally have more of a work focus on the household and immediate society whilst men give higher priority to issues outside the home.

Often men work in the formal economy with salaries and job titles — *productive*[8] work. These activities often require formal education, either as an apprentice or through the school system. Women carry out similar work, but often this is part-time, carried out at home rather than in a workplace and often it is not paid for. A (male) farmer growing a cash crop and selling it, so he can buy food, contributes to the economy and is recognised for his work. A woman growing food at home for consumption at home does not buy or sell the produce and so her activity is not recognised in the same way. Even paid jobs for women are often part-time to fit in with their other activities and are not regarded as important as 'careers' in either social status or pay levels. In formal employment, women are less likely to be in positions of authority and more likely to be doing a low-paid, unskilled menial job. Using solely economic definitions of development, such as Gross Domestic Product[9] (GDP) can lead to women's contribution being excluded. 'Voluntary' work on a development project or on a food-for-work programme also falls into this category and it is important to be aware of gender divisions in these cases. As this is a male-dominated area, any change in the commercial sector can have a disproportionate impact on men.

Men and women have *domestic*[10] roles as well as productive ones. These activities do not earn income. Domestic work includes cooking, cleaning, childcare, looking after the sick and elderly and managing domestic expenditure. This work is important for the standard of living of the whole household and is normally carried out by women. More affluent households can afford labour-saving devices, domestic help and access to other resources to reduce this burden. This shifts the domestic duties so that they become other people's productive work – although usually low-paid. Men often have a smaller domestic role, perhaps being responsible for the capital activities (e.g. house building/maintenance) and issues like security. These domestic roles are passed from mother to daughter, father to son.

---

8. Productive — or commercial, or economic. Domestic work is also productive and economic, so commercial is perhaps the more accurate term.
9. GDP — the market value of all goods and services produced within a country's borders.
10. Domestic roles are sometimes called reproductive, but this can cause confusion with the biological act of child bearing. Many domestic duties are divided socially, not biologically, and are not fixed.

"...in the transition economies of Eastern Europe, increases in women's life expectancies relative to men's in the 1990's were the result not of improvements in female longevity but of increases in male mortality. These increases reflect biological and social factors, including high work-related stress and rising rates of unemployment, smoking, and alcohol consumption. Such phenomena affect the well-being not only of men but of their families and society."

Engendering Development — Through Gender Equality In Rights, Resources and Voice, World Bank (2001)

The focus of these domestic activities is the household, so facilities that everybody requires, are not deemed 'public' infrastructure and can be given a lower priority than more visible investments. This can make a difference to the lives of women. On-plot sanitation is personal and domestic, but a road is for the community and productive. People also have another,

community role. Within the family, a woman is a mother, daughter or sister, with defined responsibilities towards other members of the family. Within the wider community, her work in and around the home provides the links with neighbours that create social cohesion. Some of this social networking such as committee work, is obvious, but other mechanisms may not be apparent to an outsider. Discussion about social issues often takes place around the local water source for women or over a drink for men. This may appear to be idle conversation, but can be an important part of building and maintaining community links. Men's community work, such as membership of local councils, is often more publicly acknowledged and discussion takes place in a central, more formal manner. Community work can be paid, but consider the status of public service jobs such as nursing (largely female) and the police or military (largely male).

Everybody also has *personal* activities, such as washing and personal hygiene, often taught by a mother to her children.

Who cleans the latrine?

Any piece of infrastructure requires somebody to operate and maintain it — there is no maintenance-free option. This applies to household latrines as well as major water treatment works. This needs to be recognised in the design. A smooth floor and access to water can make cleaning easier. This task is not pleasant and often ends up being the duty of somebody at the bottom of the social scale — women, 'sweepers'* or school children.

Should children be cleaning latrines or studying?
Managers of infrastructure have to decide what it is aiming to achieve.

* In India, sweepers are the group of people who collect rubbish and empty bucket latrines. They have a very low social status.

Infrastructure for men and infrastructure for women

The analysis of people's roles can be extended to cover the way they use infrastructure. People use infrastructure in different ways — a long distance lorry driver and a local market trader will both use the same road, but for different amounts of time and at different frequencies. Designing a road just to meet the needs of the lorry driver will not necessarily suit the market trader and not benefit the whole of society — with the costs[11] that could entail. If the majority of lorry drivers are men and small-scale market traders are women, then the analysis takes on another dimension.

Physical infrastructure can be used by men and women to improve their lives commercially, domestically, socially and personally. The way in which it is built can also have an impact. The impact can be *commercial*, as men and women are employed to design and construct the infrastructure, gaining income, training and experience. Formal design and construction have tended to be seen as male-dominated activities, although women are more often involved in the more menial tasks, such as carrying loads. However, there are some longer-term impacts.

---

11. *Costs* include the existing or potential benefits that are lost due to the proposed action. Thus if a new reservoir is built, the costs are not just the building costs, but the lost opportunities for any existing fishing, water supply and farming activities that will be disrupted and the lost benefits that the money that was used for the dam could have otherwise been spent on.

As women are the main stakeholders in an improved water system, there has long been a call for them to be involved in water projects. Participative projects provide a mixture of training, public responsibility, sense of worth and experience of decision-making, which in turn enables women to take on other *community* or *commercial* roles. Thus water supplies can be a catalyst or focus for something more than just health improvements or a reduction in chores. Employment in the design and construction process moves a participative project from having an indirect impact on their commercial activities to direct benefits.

Socio-economic analyses looking at inequalities of opportunity between men and women tend to concentrate on issues such as education, political representation, legal rights and economic status. Analysing the impacts of infrastructure developments on the community requires planners to look at the use of the infrastructure by men and women. This needs sociologists to work with engineers to analyse transport patterns, agricultural activity or water use by men, women and children.

More than just construction

"I had to work very hard as a helper and the contractors would abuse me and also pay me little for my work. Now I can build a latrine myself and earn Rs 150 a day. I am master of myself. I have more dignity, respect and am proud of my improved status in the community"

Female mason quoted by T. Mathew, in *Waterlines*, 1998

Who builds what?

Construction practices may vary between regions within a country. An engineer from northern Uganda (where women would not help construct a building) was shocked to see women in Southwest Uganda as part of a team constructing a protected spring. Culturally women from the cattle-owning groups in the Southwest would cultivate fields and maintain the house whilst the men would be away tending cattle.

Patrick Nyeko, DWD, Uganda

Near Soroti, in eastern Uganda, men would build the walls of a house and the women would build the roof.

Joseph Oriono Eyatu, DWD, Uganda

Lasting impact

A 1991 food for work programme in Zambia provided construction training for both men and women.

One woman (with no formal qualifications) went on to be employed on the project and then subsequently by the ILO as a trainer of small contractors on a rural roads project. Another woman formed her own small contracting group of poor women and continued to seek out and get small items of work for many years after the project ended. Her group was still working when this publication was being prepared.

Sarah House

2

Why address the needs of men and women?

Poverty eradication is a primary development goal. Some 70 per cent* of the world's poor are women, and lack of access to basic services (water, sanitation, energy, transport) is exacerbating this gender divide. Focusing on women's needs alone is not the answer. Unless infrastructure programmes attend to the combined needs of women and men, they risk reinforcing the inequitable distribution of work and resources that already play such an important part in female poverty.

Chapter 2 makes the case for an inclusive approach to infrastructure development to help break the cycles of deprivation and poverty. It shows how engineers can balance the needs of all sections of society and provide infrastructure that will foster a reduction in societal inequalities.

The key points are:

- Men's and women's needs have to be considered together, if a balanced and lasting solution is to be reached.

- Meeting the needs of all sections of society makes best use of available financial, human and physical resources, as well as contributing to international goals for social justice and poverty eradication.

- Participative and inclusive projects are more effective in meeting targets and more sustainable.

- Basing infrastructure provision on existing male/female stereotypes is likely to perpetuate inequalities; more equitable burden sharing can be encouraged by gender-sensitive approaches.

- Redressing past neglect of women's perspectives may require a positive bias towards them, but must not lead to discrimination against men.

* A figure commonly used from the *UNDP Human Development Report*, 1995

An engineering concern?

To many engineers, correcting inequities in society and advancing the status of women are the responsibilities of others. Their professional qualification and training equips them to design and construct infrastructure to meet terms of reference set by 'the client'. Social engineering is the remit of politicians; civil engineers are concerned with the physical structures necessary to meet goals specified by others.

True as this traditional perspective may be, it is not the end of the story. Today's engineer has to recognise the connectivity of social and physical development and the way that user acceptance influences the ultimate success of an engineering project. Today's 'clients' encompass the whole community affected by an infrastructure improvement and meeting their needs should be seen as an implicit part of the project brief. Participatory[12] design is becoming standard practice in development programmes. Fully inclusive participation is the doorway to equity and sustainability. It may mean working with other specialists in community mobilisation and participatory planning. It does not mean passing to others the responsibility for ensuring that the project benefits men and women, rich and poor.

There are a variety of reasons for addressing the needs of different groups in society when providing infrastructure. These vary from pragmatic economic issues to a consideration of human rights.

Effectiveness and efficiency

If the purpose of public infrastructure is for the use and convenience of society, then it should be useful and convenient for everybody. Providing a service for only a proportion of the target group is an inefficient use of resources. Constructing infrastructure for it to be poorly used or fall quickly into disrepair because it cannot be maintained sustainably (due to a lack of skills, finance or motivation) is a waste of time, effort and scarce funds.

Involving prospective users has practical impacts — locals are more likely to know where natural resources are, such as sand or building stone; they are able to supply historical information, such as flow rates or flooding patterns. Sometimes this knowledge is restricted to small groups — so if you want to know about the reliability of a spring, ask the people who visit it everyday to collect water.

---

12. Participatory: where groups and individuals are given opportunities to be involved in aspects of a project's process.

"I was brought up in the city of Pune. My parents were quite unorthodox in their approach to menstruation and I did not have to endure exclusion from religious functions, or seclusion at home and elsewhere and so on during my periods. But I did face a major problem — attendance at school. It was about 7km away from my home and commuting was not direct; hence I could not come home easily if I had a problem at school. The school was located in an area with very little groundwater, and the municipal water supply was also inadequate. As a result, on most days, all taps in the school, including those in the toilets, ran dry. I needed to change every 4 to 5 hours for about 3 to 4 days and hence I had to remain absent from school at the beginning of each period — which lasted for 9 or 10 days. One or two of my teachers were concerned about the gaps in my attendance and I distinctly remember two occasions on which I was asked why I remained absent so often. Unfortunately, I did not have the courage to broach the subject myself and I remained guiltily silent, as if I had no valid reason, and accepted the blame."

A real life case study reported by Kalpavriksh, a Pune based NGO, quoted in *Menstrual Hygiene and Management in Developing Countries: Taking Stock*, 2004, Sowmyaa Bharadwaj and Archana Patkar, Junction Social, Mumbai, India

There is also the question of synergy with other developmental goals. If projects are meant to support the international development targets aimed at reducing poverty, then the needs of the poor should be given priority, in order to maximise impact in meeting these goals.

Rights and policy

Ignoring the needs of groups of society is also an issue of human rights — people must not be denied access to publicly provided services just because they are poor or women. International and national policies have been drawn up to try and ensure that the rights of vulnerable groups are respected and people are treated equitably.

Equity

Men and women carry out different jobs, with different needs and priorities, often related to their traditional roles. They also have other socially determined differences:

• different levels of access to resources — from education to physical infrastructure;

"The state may not unfairly discriminate directly or indirectly against anyone on one or more grounds, including race, gender, sex, pregnancy, marital status, ethnic or social origin, colour, sexual orientation, age, disability, religion, conscience, belief, culture, language, and birth."

South African Constitution, Chapter 2, Section 9, paragraph 3, 8/5/1996

Who should engineers talk to?

"A local development programme protected a spring in a village. On a visit to the village at a later date, some of the women were asked whether they were happy with the work. They replied that they were not as the protection had been undertaken on the wrong spring. The one developed dries up in the dry season whereas another one on the other side of the village flows all year. They obviously had not been consulted in the planning stage."

Lila Pieters, from a project in Bukavu, Zaire

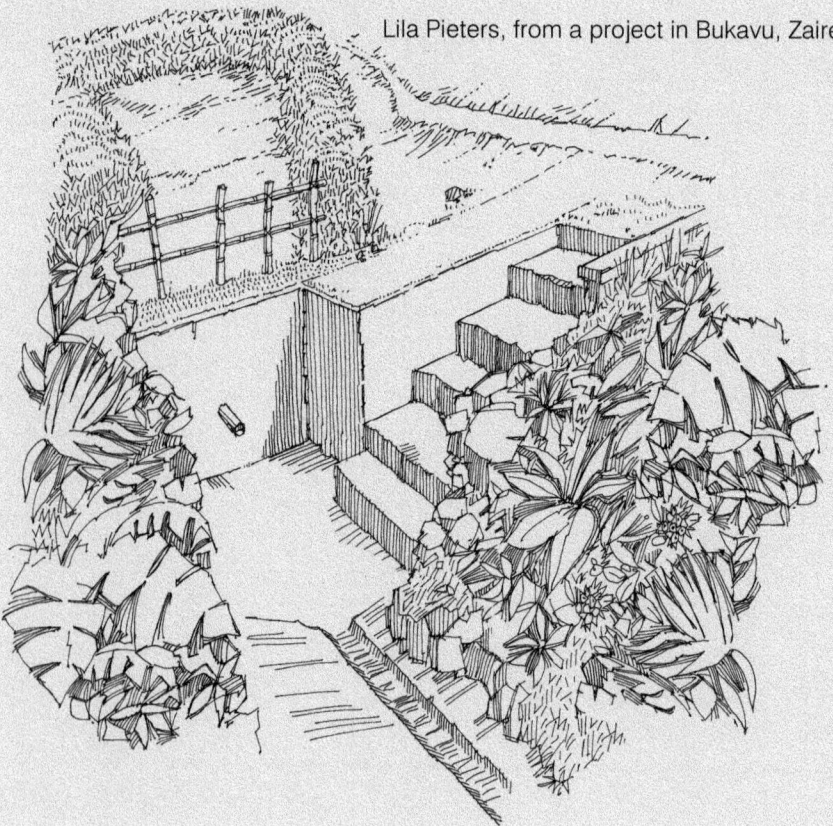

- different levels of authority and influence at all levels of formal and informal government; and

- different legal status and protection under the law.

These disparities become more extreme amongst the poor. Girls in poor families are less likely to go to school than their brothers, but this discrimination is markedly less in households that are more affluent.[13]

Addressing issues of equality does not mean that everybody has to act the same but that men and women, rich and poor should be equal in terms of:

- opportunities (equal pay for equal work, equal access to resources and education);

- their voice – having a say in formal and informal decision-making; and

- the law.

Participation = Effectiveness

In an analysis of 121 water projects, it was found that there was a strong correlation between overall project effectiveness and overall beneficiary participation*.

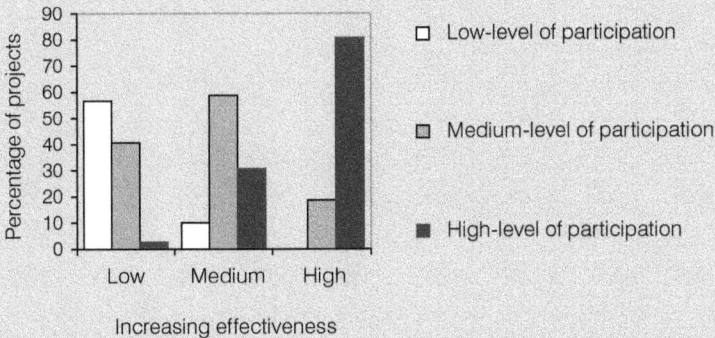

The Contribution of People's Participation —Evidence from
121 Rural Water Supply Projects, Deepa Narayan, World Bank (1995)

* See the appendix for the statistical basis of these correlations

---

13. *Engendering Development – Through Gender Equality in Rights, Resources and Voice* (2001) World Bank Policy Research Report.

Human rights legislation is generally based on the premise that men and women should be given access to the resources and live in a society where they are free to make their own choices about what life they wish to lead. Addressing inequalities is an aspect of development in its own right. As well as the absolute measures of wealth, health and education, the disparities between the rich and poor, men and women are indicators of the standard of living in a society. Engineering developments can have positive or negative impacts on existing inequalities and it is up to the engineer to make the impacts positive.

Why women in particular?

Gender policies and rights have developed for sound developmental, economic, practical and social reasons. These are often lost in the rhetoric that surrounds the issues.

There are many disadvantaged groups in society, as people are discriminated against on grounds of sex, income, race, religion, sexuality and physical ability. Even grouping people in this way ignores the fact that rich women may not be excluded but poor disabled men are. However, providing infrastructure to meet individual needs is usually impractical and anyway may disguise shared concerns.

Fifty per cent of society

Women are half of society, so addressing their needs should be a must on numerical grounds alone. Excluding half of the population from using infrastructure because it has been designed only for the taller, heavier or stronger half of the population is bad product design, giving a poor return on the investment. Women are the majority users of properly designed latrines, because of their greater concerns over privacy. Therefore, to design sanitation without considering the needs of women when they are menstruating or pregnant is poor engineering because it fails to meet the needs of more than half of the prospective users for major periods of their lives. The proportion of women users may be much larger in some areas, such as refugee camps or regions where a high proportion of male migrants have moved away to find work.

Efficiency

For many tasks, women and girls have socially determined roles. For example, they are predominantly responsible for collecting water and have to look after members of the family when they are sick. A safe,

reliable, convenient water supply therefore has a major impact on their lives. Designing a water supply with women in mind ensures that it meets their needs. Involving them in management and maintenance also ensures that the people looking after the system have a vested interest in keeping it operating. Services will only flourish if they provide a product that people are willing and able to pay for. If women are responsible for water collection, they will be the main group with an interest in keeping it running, providing it meets their needs. If it does not provide an adequate service, then the investment is wasted.

Poverty reduction

It is not just physical issues that need to be considered. Economic and social factors have been ignored in the past. The poor are often excluded because they have little political or economic influence. A higher proportion of poor people are women and a poor woman will often have less influence on society than her husband. Female-headed households tend to be particularly poor and vulnerable. Poverty-reduction projects therefore need to ensure that the needs of poor women are addressed if they are to have an impact. If a project wants to reach all of society, it should ensure that the poorest, most excluded people have access. If they can benefit from the intervention, then so should groups with fewer disadvantages.

Economic impact

Women are usually responsible for the household economy, producing, buying and preparing food, looking after children, old people and the sick. Improving women's lives, women's health, and women's economic status will impact not just on them, but the whole household — making an efficient channel for resources to the whole of society. This responsibility for the household often means women have more work to do than men — for example working during the day with men and then coming home to start the domestic chores. Meeting the needs of these women can improve their lives and the lives of those around them.

Women are also important economically, in the formal and informal sectors. In investment terms, support to the large number of small women-led enterprises may have a more profound social and economic impact than support to more formal industrial concerns.

Women's diverse roles can mean that they do not have the time or energy to participate in project activities as much as the project team would like. Even if they are paid for their work, they still have to carry out their domestic tasks as well — or get their daughters to do the work to the detriment of school attendance.

Why not men?

'Gender' is used to describe these issues rather than 'women', as what is important is the roles of and relationships between men and women[14] in society, not just specific groups in isolation. Men need to recognise and understand women's roles so they can work together to improve inequalities[15]. Men do benefit from an improved water supply, even if they are not directly involved. Reduced sickness and improved sanitation is good for the whole community and everybody should be prepared to contribute equally.

Even when development benefits society as a whole, some groups may consider that their loss of relative advantage over other people outweighs the absolute improvement in their standard of living. Any extension of decision-making influence to previously disenfranchised groups has to be handled carefully, as powerful groups may oppose any change. The reason why women's physical and socio-economic needs have frequently been

---

14. Sometimes other gender groups are recognised, such as the Daudu in Northern Nigeria or the 30,000 'hermaphrodites' (Hirza) in Bangladesh. The different roles of children are also sometimes implied by the term 'gender'.
15. Looking at men and women's roles together is often called a 'Gender and Development' approach (GAD).

ignored in the past is due to the relative influence of men and women at policy and project levels.

Due to past neglect of women's perspectives, there needs to be a bias towards them[16], but this should not lead to exclusion of men or only considering gender issues and not those of other vulnerable groups, such as the poor or politically marginalized.

The myth of community[17]

Words like stakeholder[18], participant, beneficiary[19], agent[20], community and household can be 'gender blind' by implying that everyone so grouped is bound by common interests. For example 'farmers' may cover one group, but the needs of commercial (usually male) farmers growing crops for market will be different from subsistence (often female) farmers growing crops for use at home. Similarly 'women' may not reflect the needs of girls or widows. Within households, wives may be subject to their mothers-in-law. 'Communities' form around common interests; people may regard themselves as being in several communities at once, based on location, common beliefs or shared tasks. Heads of households may not be in charge of household tasks like collecting water, food or fuel. Female-headed households have different needs than male-headed households and are

---

16. Looking at women in isolation is often called a 'Women in (or and) Development' approach (WID or WAD).
17. See *The Myth of Community – Gender issues in participatory development*, Irene Guijt and Meera Kaul Shah, ITDG 1998.
18. A 'stakeholder' is anybody who has an interest or 'stake' in the project. This includes designers, contractors, donors as well as users, project staff and other groups of people who may benefit or suffer from the project.
19. A 'beneficiary' is anybody who (passively) benefits from a project, without necessary participating.
20. An 'agent' is anybody who takes part actively in development projects, rather than just being a passive beneficiary.

often an indicator of poverty. 'Gender' should also be used carefully; if it means 'women', the word 'women' should be used.

Taken to its extreme, an analysis of society by groups will put each individual in a group of their own. Engineers are used to grouping distinct attributes to make them easier to analyse. Aquifers, flow regimes in rivers and rock types all have their individual characteristics, but can be classified by permeability, seasonal variation or strength. Gender and economic status are significant measures of people's social standing across a wide range of societies and an analysis according to these parameters will give an initial insight into different communities.

Stereotypes and the status quo

Many of the traditional roles of women are not fixed and may vary between cultures and change over time. Assuming that it is a woman's role to collect water and designing the system around that assumption may serve to reinforce that role and lose an opportunity for change. Any engineering project will be changing the environment that society lives in. Hopefully, engineers will be improving that environment with better services and infrastructure. The construction of infrastructure will also change the cultural practices of society, altering who does what and how activities change. Unwittingly these changes can impact adversely on different sectors of society. Engineers need to be aware of this and take action to avoid negative impacts and actively improve the livelihoods of all members of society, especially those least able to influence or mitigate the changes.

In the assessment of roles, the question, who does what? should be followed by why them? Defending the poor social status of any group by invoking tradition or culture is not a valid justification. Engineers change culture when they build a road or construct a hospital; a cultural awareness and respect for traditions should not perpetuate discrimination. Dramatic changes in the social or physical infrastructure can have the power to harm as well as help society. Engineers and social scientists need to be aware that their short-term interventions will have long-term impacts.

Every stakeholder will have their own perceptions about who normally carries out certain tasks. These do not only vary from place to place but can change over time. Engineers need to be aware of their own preconceived opinions and ensure they do not limit the use of infrastructure to only one social group, for example washing clothes can be carried out by men and women, so the design of washing slabs should suit both groups.

3

For the use and convenience of society

Meeting the needs of the client is a basic part of any engineering project. When the project is to improve public infrastructure, the 'client' encompasses a range of people, often referred to as stakeholders. They include different groups of direct users, but also politicians, associations, NGOs*, utilities and private organisations that may be affected in one way or another by the new developments.

Between them, the promoter and the engineer need to ensure that all the stakeholders have a chance to express views and participate in decisions. This chapter looks at ways in which the engineer can collect and analyse information and tailor the infrastructure to meet the needs of all. One of the critical divisions may often be the different needs of men and women. Gender perspectives are therefore crucially important.

Key points in Chapter 3 are:

*   People can shape infrastructure if they are involved in its development. Enabling them to participate effectively requires special skills. Engineers and sociologists need to work together to ensure that the infrastructure reflects everyone's needs.

*   Indicators of the involvement of men and women in development projects have to be selected carefully. Measuring outcomes in numeric terms may be misleading; gender equity relates more to equality of opportunity than balanced committee membership.

*   The engineer can produce practical responses that also have strategic implications (improving gender equity, combating poverty, etc.).

*NGO – non-governmental organization.

An engineering design can only be as good as the data on which it is based. That is just as true for socio-economic data as it is for geological, hydrological and meteorological data. Each society is different and engineers can adapt infrastructure to meet the needs of the different groups, once those needs have been suitably defined. The standard approach is to:

- gather data on the different uses of infrastructure by men and women (and other social groups)[21];
- analyse the data; and
- act on the findings of the data analysis.

In an inclusive participatory programme, each of these stages is undertaken with the active involvement of appropriate stakeholders. This is not a concession or a reduction in the engineer's expert role; the sustainability of the completed project will depend on the sense of ownership developed through the participatory process. Also, participation should not be taken for granted. People are being asked to devote time and energy that are in short supply. They need to perceive that it will be in their interests to contribute. The ways that information is delivered to different groups is important, and some motivational expertise has to be applied to generate enthusiasm for participation.

Therefore it is necessary to collect and analyse data on the stakeholders, noting that there will be variations from community to community and within communities.

Measuring inequalities

Some of the social indicators[22] that have been used in the past have been crude and do not necessarily measure the impact that infrastructure can have on the lives of men and women, for example:

- The number of men and women on management committees; this is easy to measure, but does the committee have authority over all decisions about infrastructure development? Are the women on the committee able to voice their concerns? Are the women well-educated, articulate, related to influential men? Who represents the poor?
- The involvement of women in construction. 'Voluntary' labour is more

---

21. Sometimes this is called 'disaggregated' data.
22. Indicators are objective ways of measuring that progress is being achieved, and must relate to the aims and objectives of the project or piece of work. Gosling and Edwards, *Toolkits*, Save the Children, 1995.

likely to be carried out by poor people than the rich. Voluntary labour can add extra burdens to women, who already have no spare time.

- The number of female engineers on a project. Although women may have better access to women's groups than men and may have an empathy with some of their concerns, this does not mean they are more aware or able to respond to gender issues. Female engineers go through the same training as their male counterparts.

- The saving of time or increased economic benefits for women. If the time saved is taken up by extra work or the money earned goes on household expenditure, the position of women relative to men may not have altered.

The numbers of women committee members or female engineers are only measurements of some of the methods that can be used to ensure an equitable engineering project. The measurements that are most important are not the tools used, but the impact they have. The length of pipe laid on a project only has an impact if water reaches the user; the number of women on a committee only has an impact if they can make meaningful decisions about the whole project and this results in a better service. Impacts may be economic (reduced cost of water), physical (reduced burden), environmental (reduced pollution) or personal (increased health) and these in turn can have social impacts.

Technical indicators may include the amount of water collected, improved water quality through hygienic practices, improved health, reduced time and distance to collect water, level of tariffs and collection rates. This can be disaggregated to see who is collecting water, who is paying tariffs and who is maintaining latrines. It is this engineering-related data that will be used to judge the success of an infrastructure project. It is important that if equality issues are to be considered by engineers, the indicators used to measure impact of a project should relate primarily to the technical outputs and then consider the affect that this has on the various parts of the community.

Indicators should reflect equality of opportunity, not equality of outcome. Just looking at the outcomes may mean that social inclusion is forced (e.g. women having to attend meetings when they would prefer to be doing something else). The absolute status needs to be assessed, as equality between men and women may mean neither group has a good standard of living.

In a pilot study for a poverty impact assessment, small surveys were carried out in several towns in Uganda. The following indicators looked at access to water and sanitation services.

Indicators	Jinja	Lira	Mbarara	Tororo
% of households (h/hs) with their own pipe connection	37	0	25	22
Average consumption litres/capita/day	21	26	30	35
Average hours of utility water supply per day	16	12.8	22	13
Average days per week that utility water is supplied	5.7	6.9	6	6
Average time to collect water each day (minutes)	110	271	26	90
Average distance to nearest usable piped water	29	122	92	108
% of h/hs who buy water from a neighbour	11	5	65	48
% of h/hs using water kiosks or standposts	52	85	0	26
% of h/hs who use more than one source	67	35	55	48
% of water collected by women and by children	84.5	56% women and 43% children	82.5	92
Average monthly water bill (Ugandan Shillings)	8000	7536	8540	15440
% of people satisfied with utility services	26	30	30	61
% with functioning sanitation within 20 m	89	70	75	83

Source: Uganda Urban Poverty Survey 2003

Which of these indicators has the biggest social impact if improved – time, water availability or cost? Only by enabling women to make meaningful technical decisions on priorities can the service provision be improved. The key indicator will be the improvement in service, not how it was achieved.

Note that the disaggregated data (women and children) on who collects water gives more information than the combined figure, with technical and socio-economic implications.

37

Measuring water quality can move beyond counting coliforms and look at how people manage water in the home. A study in Zambia showed that the quality of water changed between point of collection and point of use.

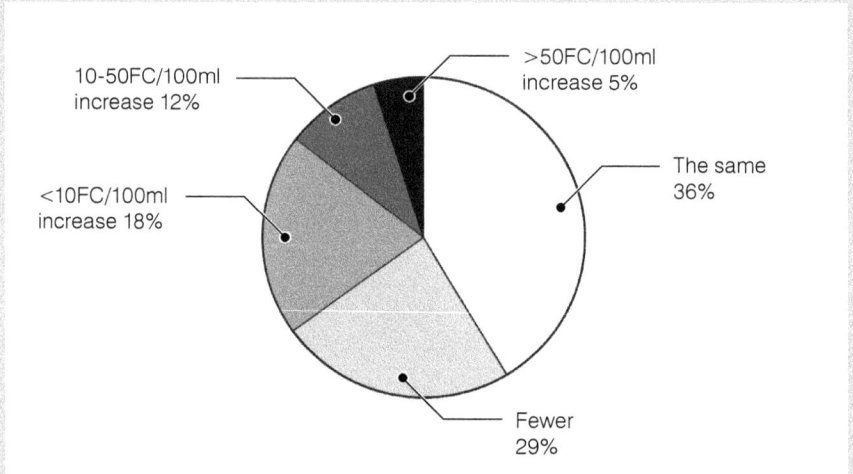

Pie chart:
- 10-50FC/100ml increase 12%
- >50FC/100ml increase 5%
- <10FC/100ml increase 18%
- The same 36%
- Fewer 29%

Reasons for the water quality change included:

- Containers: open bowls and buckets had more potential for contamination than plastic water containers.

- Carrying: floating a leaf or plastic bag on an open bowl reduces water slopping out, but can contaminate the water.

- Storage: although most people preferred freshly drawn water, 40% of households would have liked to store water for longer (to increase water use, but also increasing bacteriological die-off).

Gender roles influence this as men would make the final decision about household purchases, thus deciding if water containers were worth buying.

Water quality was also enhanced by very basic improvements to the source, to avoid having to wade into a muddy pool and scoop out water. The physical enhancement not only improved water quality, but also made collecting water more dignified and less physically challenging and thus more acceptable to men.

Sally Sutton, 27th WEDC International Conference

Consultation and participation

Responding to simple questions, as in a census, only provides limited information and does not necessarily reflect people's opinions and priorities. To discover what issues are important to men and women, they need to be asked for their opinions. It needs to be made apparent too that what they say will be taken into account and that there will be mechanisms through which they can be involved more closely in decision-making. That means 'participation'.

Participation can take many forms, with a range of involvement by the community, as Figure 3.1 illustrates.

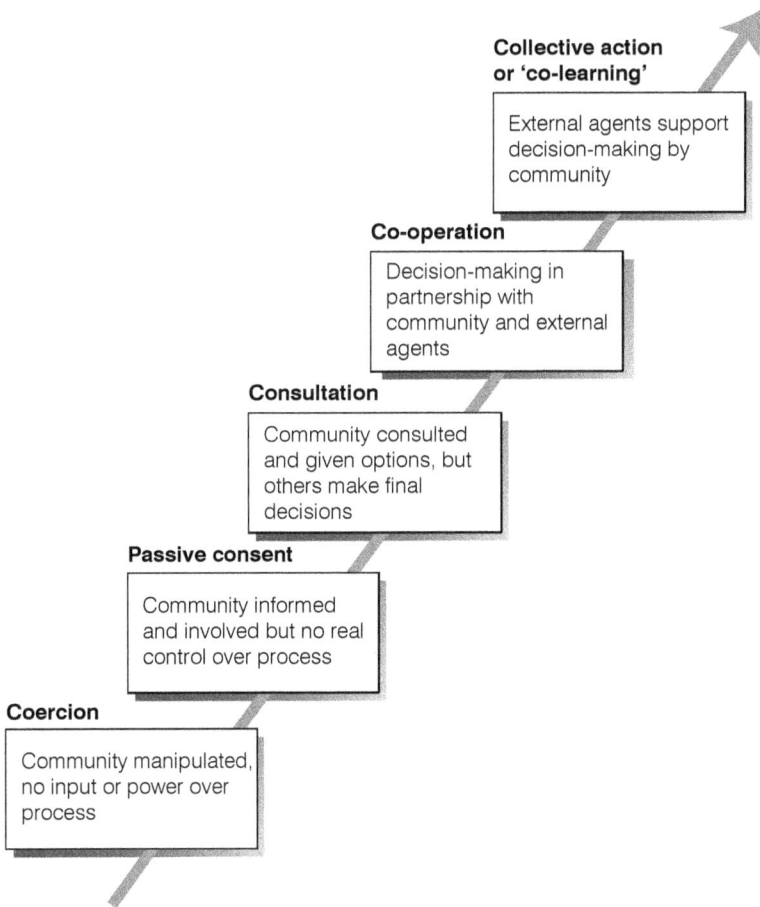

Collective action or 'co-learning'
External agents support decision-making by community

Co-operation
Decision-making in partnership with community and external agents

Consultation
Community consulted and given options, but others make final decisions

Passive consent
Community informed and involved but no real control over process

Coercion
Community manipulated, no input or power over process

Figure 3.1. Scales of participation

"A common outcome of consultation is the generation of a wish list for which those consulted have no sense of responsibility or ownership."

"Participation is about power, an increase in the power of the dis-advantaged."

(*Handbook of Social/Gender Analysis*, Coady International Institute)

Participation in the project does not just provide relevant information. If a community can identify with, and feel that they own the project, there will be a better chance of sustained operation. A full sense of ownership can only be created through participation of all actual or potential stakeholders throughout the project cycle. Everybody who is affected by a project, from whatever angle, has a right to be involved. Participation is more than simply making 'voluntary' contributions of time, effort or money. Beneficiaries should not have a passive role, just accepting what they are given. Participation means recognising all their needs and designing the project accordingly, giving users a voice and a choice.

The form that participation takes will vary with the type of project. At one end of the scale, collective action requires engineers and project managers to support rather than lead the decision-making process. This means accepting that the project is not 'owned' by the donor and the 'client' is not just the government department or NGO overseeing the project.

Engineers are familiar with the concept of sample surveys; tunnel engineers joke that the best trial hole for a bore is one slightly wider than the planned tunnel! However, it is accepted that a series of geological cores will enable a general picture of the geology to be gained that is good enough for the design of the tunnel. Site investigations always have to balance getting sufficient information to reduce the chances of unforeseen ground conditions against the cost of surveys that are too detailed and expensive.

Similarly, it is not feasible to consult with everybody in a community, so representatives have to be identified to give an idea of the range of views and opinions. If participation of representatives of all stakeholder groups is achieved this can lead to:

- improved efficiency through maximising use of local skills and knowledge;

- a project which meets the demand of all users (women, men and children);
- a greater sense of ownership;
- increased motivation to sustain the project once outside support has stopped; and
- improved transparency and accountability (fewer opportunities for corruption).

Engineers and planners should be flexible in their approaches to project development and must be prepared to listen as well as explaining the programme or asking questions. Specific strategies need to be adopted to ensure that women as well as men are given every opportunity to make their voices heard. Options include holding separate meetings for men and women or finding out how women receive information — lower levels of literacy may mean posters at a health centre may not be as effective as talking directly to women's groups.

Project participants

In a design, the engineer identifies the factors that will influence the project outcome, from financial and economic forecasts, to ground conditions and availability of physical resources. For a site investigation, the engineering geologist will examine geological maps, then may visit the sites being considered and finally, once the plans have been developed sufficiently, carry out a site investigation with boreholes or trial pits. The site investigation will continue through the design and construction phases, gathering increasingly more detailed and specific information.

The parallel socio-economic activity sets out to analyse who is involved, how closely and what their interests are. This needs to be carried out at an early stage, and, as with engineering investigation, may be repeated several times in increasing detail. It will look at generally available data,

Talking toilets

It takes a while to get people to discuss toilets, but many women readily provide personal and detailed observations. Some of the men tend to be very impersonal or make a joke about it.

Based on Clara Greed in *The Times Higher Education Supplement* 26/07/02

such as censuses and previous reports. Visits to the location and talking to representatives of various groups will follow this. The final stages will involve detailed investigations, using methods such as PRA[23], surveys and structured interviews, which will continue through the design, implementation and operation of the project. As the project progresses, more people will participate in the process, shown in Figure 3.2.

The term 'user' does not necessarily reflect everybody affected by a development. A 'stakeholder' is any person, or any group of people who may be directly or indirectly impacted by a project, either positively or negatively. This includes not only users (primary stakeholders), but also secondary stakeholders, including:

- all those who stand to benefit from the project;

- people who may not benefit directly or may be disadvantaged;

- NGOs and community-based organisations, such as farmers' associations, trades unions, women's groups or water user groups;

- government departments and agencies, and their staff;

- utilities (whether in the public or private sector) and their staff;

- private producers, local artisans and entrepreneurs;

- donors, consultants, contractors, and their staff;

- professional associations (e.g. institutions of engineers);

- schoolteachers, religious leaders and media representatives (sometimes known as 'agents for change').

- councillors and other political representatives;

- political, social and environmental campaigners; and

- schoolteachers, religious leaders and media representatives (sometimes known as 'agents for change').

If any stakeholder is not involved in the process, there may be problems at a later stage ranging from a failure to realise the full potential of the investment to active protest against the project. Participation may appear to cost a lot; non-participation can cost very much more. A parallel exists

---

23. PRA: participatory rural/rapid appraisal; a method of generating and sharing information with a community, using actions and materials that they are familiar with. For more information see *Participatory Development Tool Kit* (Narayan and Srinivasan) World Bank 1994.

with site investigations, where cutting corners on surveys can lead to extra expense later and delay due to unforeseen ground conditions.

Elements of analysis

An analysis of an engineering structure may consider several parameters such as the structural strength under the ultimate load pattern, the crack width and deflection under service load patterns and the cost. A sociological analysis will also need to look at a variety of aspects in order to build up a picture of the society. These will vary at an individual level, but there will also be general characteristics that are common to certain groups.

Sociologists have tended to analyse societies in either of two ways:

- regard the whole of society as divided into groups and these group structures determine how the community operates (structuralism[24]), or

- regard everybody as individuals, with their membership of any artificial 'group' being irrelevant to their livelihood (constructivism[25])

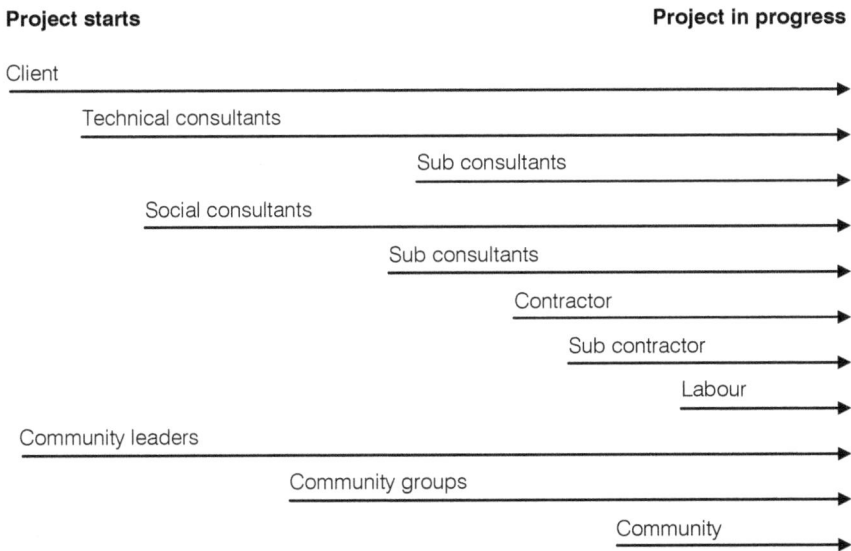

Project starts   **Project in progress**

Client

Technical consultants

Sub consultants

Social consultants

Sub consultants

Contractor

Sub contractor

Labour

Community leaders

Community groups

Community

Figure 3.2. Number of participants increases as the project cycle progresses

---

24. Structuralism: a model of society proposed by Emile Durkheim (1858–1917), where society is made up of institutions and not individuals.
25. Constructivism: a model of society proposed by Max Weber (1864–1920), where ideas like 'community' are only the result of individuals' actions.

In post-apartheid South Africa, a new group of disadvantaged people is emerging. Young white men without qualifications have to compete in the labour market for manual work with the majority black population. Traditional division of labour along racial lines excludes these men from unskilled jobs, leaving them unemployed.

Julie Fisher, WEDC/Carolien Van Der Voorden, Mvula Trust

An analysis based only on the divisions between men and women is a structuralist approach. This may miss out finer distinctions or lead to an incorrect assessment if it is assumed that, for example, a few women are representative of the whole community. The alternative focus on individuals can ignore the shared problems of a particular group (such as girls' access to education). Modern practice tends to combine the two approaches (structuration[26]), recognising that everybody is individual, but will share some concerns with a variety of people – thus one individual can be a housewife, farmer, mother, woman and poor.

The analysis often involves several iterative stages. A rapid appraisal can recognize major socio-economic groups (rich/poor, men/women) but further analysis may reveal special interests of less obvious groups (widows, landless farmers).

Engineers are used to making decisions based on many factors. Water resources analysis assesses water quantity, quality (itself based on many parameters) and the daily, annual and long-term variations of these factors in order to characterize a water source. Sociologists use a similar variety of overlapping tools to characterize a society[27].

Condition and position

Being aware of what tools sociologists use and what measurements they are taking should help engineers work with other members of a multidisciplinary team. Understanding the social and technical factors that are being assessed should enable the team to contribute to each

26. Structuration: a model of society proposed by Anthony Giddens (1938-), where institutions and individual action combine to shape society.
27. The following tools are based on 'Theoretical Perspectives on Gender and Development', edited by Jane L Parpart, M Patricia Connelly and V Eudine Barriteau. International Development Research Centre, Ottawa 2000.

others' work — even to the extent of providing each other with data and information to influence both the social and technical design and implementation.

People are not just defined by what they do, but the condition of their personal health, wealth and skills. This can provide information on their material needs (work, shelter, water, education). People are also assessed by where they fit into society, for example women's social and economic position relative to men. What are their wage levels? Do they have equal work and education opportunities? Are they subject to violence? Are they allowed to participate in decisions? The process of assessment should enable people to ascertain both the absolute and relative status of groups of men and women. The conditions of various groups are the symptoms of how that society shares resources and indicates the social positions of members of that society.

Types of work

When looking at a community, people will be involved in a range of tasks. These will include productive, domestic, community and personal activities. The value that society gives to each activity can be measured in a variety of ways, such as the status, wages or educational level of the people carrying them out. People will not just have a single role, but have several tasks, such as farmer, elder and husband.

Division of labour

The people who carry out each activity will vary – some may be done predominantly by men, others by women. They may share jobs equally or the division may vary seasonally.

Access to and control of resources

People carrying out a task need access to resources – so farmers will need land, seed, fertiliser, tools and water for irrigation. Restricted access to these resources can limit their effectiveness. People do not just need access to these resources, but control over them. If they are dependent on others, they are vulnerable to other people's actions. These resources include financial, natural, physical, social and human assets and may be shared differently between rich and poor, men and women. The relative access to these resources can be shown graphically (Figure 3.3).

Influencing factors and change

People do not live in isolation. The wider context influences their lives.

External factors include the economy, the environment, culture and religion, and politics. These can change over time (trends), vary seasonally or alter suddenly (shocks). Some factors are not easy to influence (climate, population growth, religion) whilst others can be addressed more readily (institutional reform, private sector involvement, legal issues, culture). The poor are more vulnerable to external factors impacting on their lives.

Potential for transformation

The development process is not static. It is worthwhile looking at the history of a community and its potential for change. In order to assess how closely people can be involved in an engineering project, it is useful to see how people participate in other activities. They may be passive recipients of benefits or take an active role in the provision of services. The potential depends on the condition and position of the powerless and the powerful. Conflict may arise if transformation threatens people's interests.

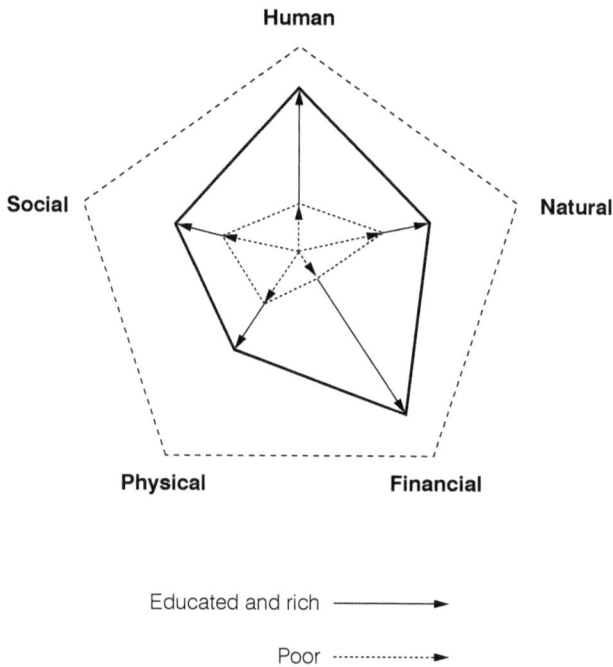

Figure 3.3. Relative access to resources*

* This diagram is often used in sustainable livelihood approaches to development, to show the multi-dimensional nature of assets. Sometimes more than five assets are identified. The rich have access to more assets than the poor — not just financial, but social (e.g. political influence), human (health and education), physical (better housing and services) and natural (cleaner air, less flooding).

A group of men return from a gender-analysis exercise in a rural African village. They show their trainer diagrams representing analyses carried out by groups of women and men in the community. The diagrams highlight the hardships faced by adolescent men. The team has not done it properly, the trainer tells them. This is not gender analysis, she says, they have got it all wrong.

Usually gender prejudice is seen as a peculiarly male problem. Yet, as this example shows, women's gender prejudices can be just as blinding. When gender analysis reveals that young men may actually be the ones at the bottom of the heap, challenges are posed to received wisdom about gender.

Andrea Cornwall in *Myth of Community,* Gujit and Shah, 1998

The gathering of socio-economic data on the condition and position of individuals and groups, and looking at the potential for transformation should then influence the design and implementation of the project or programme — in social, economic and technical ways. This process of assessment, analysis and subsequent action is shown as a flow chart in Figure 3.4. An emerging challenge is how an engineer responds to socio-economic information and the planned social transformations, and what actions can be taken.

The engineer's response

Engineers have technical responsibilities but they also have a role in the wider project team and are members of society. Engineers respond most fully in a technical manner, but they also contribute as part of the project team and as part of public duty. The two elements of the social analysis that provide information that the engineer can respond to are the condition and the position of poor men and women in a community. These can be addressed in two ways:

- practical solutions can reduce the burden of 'women's work', improve living conditions and increase access to resources; and

- longer-term strategic measures can be designed to give men and women, rich and poor more equal opportunities to an acceptable position in society.

The engineers' main role has always been to provide practical responses to the needs of society. Engineers have the skills and ability to meet this

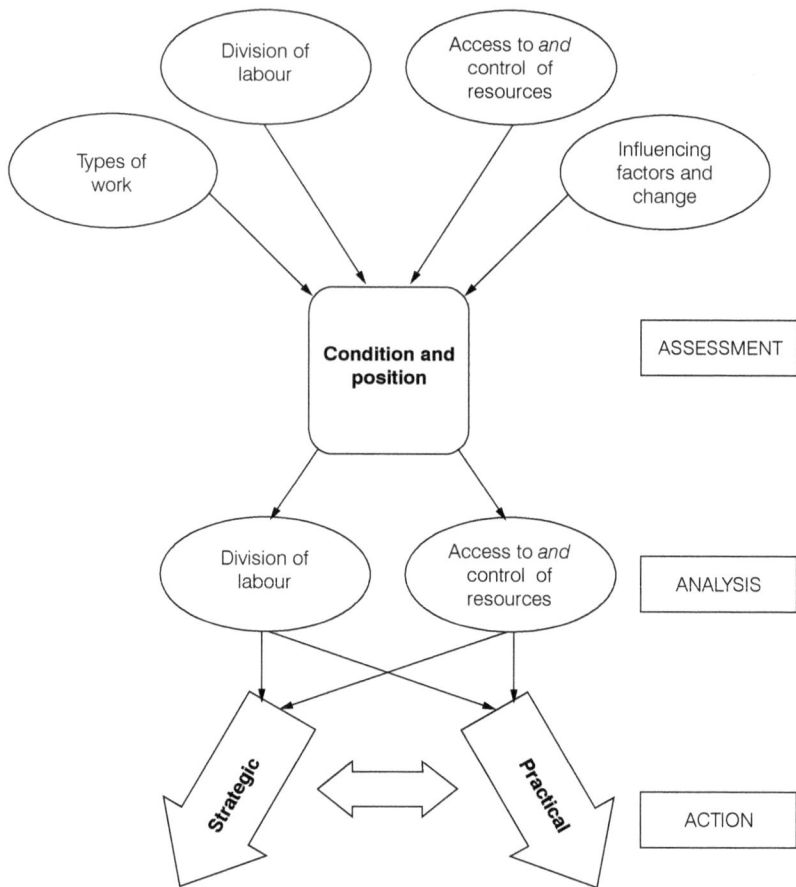

Figure 3.4. Assessment, analysis and action

Transforming communities but not technologies

Participatory Hygiene and Sanitation Transformation (PHAST) approach to water and sanitation projects is designed to promote hygiene, sanitation improvements and community management of water and sanitation facilities. However, in a project to bring water supply and sanitation improvements to peri-urban Lusaka, the representatives of the local community had been transformed into an articulate, dynamic group, but the water supply appeared to be a standard textbook design, with little acknowledgement of the community's needs, leaving the technical management of the water supply in the hands of experts.

Brian Reed and Rose Lidonde, WEDC

challenge, although in the past the physical needs of society have not necessarily been analysed according to the needs of the socially excluded. The practical responses to meet the needs of poor women will vary from those traditionally provided in two aspects:

- the product will be different, with more appropriate technologies and design details that meet the social and physical needs of men and women; and

- the process will be different, with a greater involvement by men and women in developing and implementing the infrastructure.

Engineers need an understanding of the strategic issues, so they can:

- Ensure that the infrastructure does not make women's social position worse (e.g. targeting irrigation projects at men, thus depriving women of an opportunity for income generation). New infrastructure will change society and engineers have a responsibility to make sure that costs and benefits are shared fairly.

- Work with social scientists to address problems of social exclusion. Engineers will be working in the community and this can provide opportunities not open to social scientists or normally blocked by social convention. Infrastructure projects based around improving physical conditions can evolve, with a change in focus from a practical response to a strategic action, providing an 'entry point' for other professionals. Examples include water supply projects that have been extended to provide health education or training in income-generating activities.

- Show socially responsible work practices by example, through the conduct of the engineering organization.

Pump mechanics

"The choice of women as pump mechanics was surprising to many people in Busia. It didn't occur to a man that a woman can know what he knows or learn anything"

"The spanner was a shock. I never knew in my whole life I would hold a spanner".

Quoted from women pump attendants in Busia District, Kenya, in *World Water Vision; Results of the Gender Mainstreaming Project – a Way Forward,* (2000)

The divide between practical and strategic responses is blurred. Practical improvements to people's lives require them to be willing and able to make use of the new facilities. Women do not only require training to maintain hand pumps, they need to be encouraged and supported so they have the confidence to attend the training and then carry out the task. Strategic actions, such as increased education for girls, can only be achieved if some of the practical burdens, such as collecting water, are reduced so they can take advantage of the opportunities. The two responses need to proceed together, despite the different time scale and focus, as shown in Table 3.1.

Social responsibility

Engineers can tailor their work to meet the requirements of people to ensure that the practical aspects of their work help all sectors of society. However,

Table 3.1. Comparison of practical needs and strategic interests of women*

Practical needs	Strategic interests
Tend to be immediate, short-term	Tend to be long-term
Are unique to particular women, according to the roles assigned to them in the division of labour in their society	May be viewed as being relevant to all women (e.g. all women experience some inequality relative to men, but the degree varies by class, race, religion, age, etc.)
Relate to daily needs; food, housing, income, health, children, safety	Relate to disadvantaged position; subordination, lack of resources and education, vulnerability to poverty and violence, etc.
Are easily identified by women	Are not always identifiable (e.g. women may be unaware of the basis of disadvantage or potential for change)
Can be addressed by providing specific inputs; food, hand pumps, clinics etc.	Can be addressed by consciousness-raising, increasing self-confidence, providing education, strengthening women's organisations, enabling political actions, etc.
Addressing practical needs Tends to involve women as beneficiaries and perhaps as participants Can improve the condition of women's lives Generally, does not alter traditional roles and relationships	Addressing strategic interests Involves women as agents or enables women to become agents Can improve the position of women in society Can empower women and transform gender relations and attitudes

*After Connelly et al, in *Theoretical perspectives on gender and development, (ed Parpart et al.)* International Development Research Centre, 2000, based on Moffat et al. *Two halves make a whole: balancing gender relations in development,* Canadian Council for International Co-operation (1991).

In a programme, women had been trained, organized and registered as a co-operative of masons and hand-pump mechanics with the local municipal corporation. During the project period there was ample work opportunities for these women and the claims of women's empowerment appeared relevant. An evaluation of the same co-operatives five years later revealed that they had become completely neglected and they were no longer functioning. The women explained that when the project staff left, they were unable to compete with the close bond that re-emerged between male contractors and the municipal corporation staff. The municipal corporation staff mentioned that most of the male contractors are local organised crime leaders and, with the veil of the project lifted, they could no longer afford to ignore these powerful men.

Deepa Joshi, Southampton University

providing infrastructure that meets the needs of vulnerable groups may not be enough if cultural issues limit their access in other ways. Although practical work may increase the well-being of people[28], it may miss out on the opportunities for strengthening people's access to other resources, such as social status or employment opportunities.

Work to bring about a strategic change in the position of socially excluded groups is a challenge. Although the time scale and skills required might not appear to fit within a standard infrastructure development project, there are contributions that engineers can make:

- First, do no harm. Engineers should be aware of the social status of various groups in a community and should not make their access to infrastructure or other resources worse.

- Avoid perpetuating exclusion. Just concentrating on women's role in domestic duties such as water collection, may mean that men cannot take a role in such tasks in the future.

- Be aware of who the client is — is it the funder or the user? What is the project for — long-term development or a short-term construction project?

- Communicate with the community in appropriate manners – in language, places and at times that are appropriate to different groups in society.

---

28. This is sometimes called a 'welfare' approach.

- Include all groups in the engineering process. Pro-poor employment practices can have practical and social benefits[29].

- Investigate what the barriers are to using water supplies, sanitation or fuel. Investments will be wasted if the physical infrastructure cannot be used due to other (social) factors.

- Work with others to promote a steadily more equitable society. Engineers will need to understand social objectives and be flexible in responding to any socio-economic factors

- Ensure good employment practices within their own organizations.

Sustaining social change — a success

In a study over ten years in Zambia, a ten percent rise in water collection by men mirrored a similar drop in the amount of water collected by women. It is suggested that this had less to do with changing social attitudes and more to do with a change from carrying water in bowls and buckets (which were carried on the head) to carrying water in plastic jerry cans (which can be carried on bicycles, wheelbarrows or carts). Similarly water sources used to require people wading into them to collect water but these have now been improved. It was not seemly for men to carry buckets on their head or wade into the muddy water.

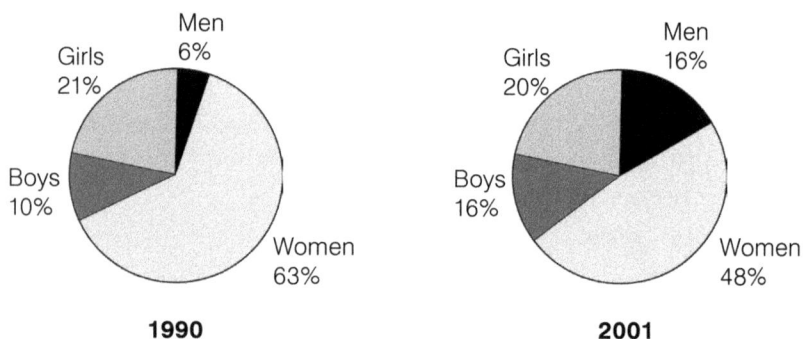

Men 6%
Girls 21%
Boys 10%
Women 63%

1990

Men 16%
Girls 20%
Boys 16%
Women 48%

2001

Sally Sutton, WEDC International Conference, 2001

---

29. For more information see *Implementing Labour Standards in Construction – a sourcebook*, Ladbury, Cotton and Jennings, WEDC 2003.

4

Participation
in the project process[30]

Civil engineering projects follow a well established progression of conception, feasibility study, design, construction, operation and maintenance and, usually, evaluation. In development programmes, the process is seen as a cycle with future extensions or follow-up projects benefiting from the evaluation phase. To gain the benefits of stakeholder participation, the traditional concept of handovers from planner to consultant to contractor to user at different stages needs to be revisited. Continuous involvement of users and other stakeholders changes the resource requirements and the timing of project phases in participatory projects compared with those of conventional civil engineering projects. Each phase has its own opportunities for engineers to foster socially inclusive infrastructure development. Key points in Chapter 4 are:

- Projects may contractually be one-off events but still need to be seen as part of the development cycle.

- The funder, the promoter or the user may be viewed as the client. The engineer needs to maintain dialogues with all stakeholders and programming should include time and resources for participation.

- Client acceptance of 'participation' does not necessarily result in the involvement of socially excluded people. Special steps may have to be taken to make the project fully inclusive.

- Projects may just concentrate on women's issues or integrate them into the main part of the infrastructure development.

- The project's outputs are not just *what* is produced, but also *how* it is produced.

---

30. In project management, 'process' means the way the project is implemented, as opposed to the engineering sense where 'treatment process' has a specific technical meaning.

Delivering the service

Design and procurement processes vary on different civil engineering projects. For example, design and build or Build, Own, Operate, Transfer (BOOT) schemes are different from the more conventional consultant/contractor method of project procurement, although the physical result is the same. Most designs start with an outline brief stating what the promoter of the work requires. If the needs of socially excluded people are going to be taken into account, they need to be involved from the start of the process.

If a project aims to contribute to improved access to rights, resources and representation for poor men and women, their contribution has to go beyond providing data. The community has to participate in decision-making, transferring skills and building up confidence. Conventional patterns of project programming have to be adapted to ensure that the way in which engineers design and construct infrastructure does not exclude people from genuine participation.

The view of the process of the development of infrastructure depends on the perspective of the viewer.

- To a person who has not been involved in the process of developing or building it, it is a single event. One day there was no water, the next day the water flowed.

- To an engineer it is a linear progression, from feasibility study through design and construction, a period of months or years. Thus it is often viewed as a flow chart.

- To the planner and policy-maker, the process is a continuous sequence, moving hopefully to improved services for the whole community. This is often portrayed as a cycle.

Project programmes normally show *what* happens and *when*, in order that activities take place in the most efficient order. The following programme charts look at *who* is involved and to what extent.

In conventional civil engineering, the promoter (client, employer) will engage a consultant to plan and design a project, which will be built by a contractor (who may use sub-contractors) and handed back to the promoter for operation. If the project is for public infrastructure, the promoter (government or private concession) will operate the service on behalf of the public (Figure 4.1a).

In many development projects the project is handed over to the community or user group rather than the promoter (donor, government, NGO) (Figure 4.1b). In a participative project, the users will be involved before handover, although the timing and amount of involvement may vary (Figure 4.1c).

These different scenarios show a shift in control from the promoter to the user, which requires the promoter to be willing to let go of control and for the user to be able and willing to take on this responsibility.

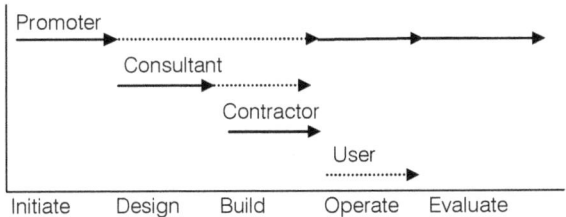

(a) Project participants: conventional project

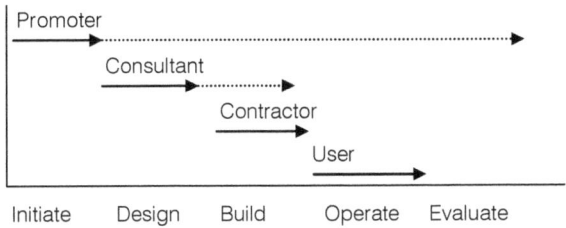

(b) Project participants: user-managed project

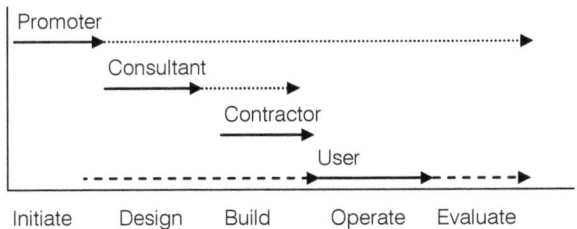

(c) Project participants: participative project

Based on Figure 5a in Principles of Engineering Organization, 2nd ed., S. Wearne, Thomas Telford, London, 1993. Full involvement is shown with a solid line, reduced involvement with a dotted line.

Figure 4.1. Project control scenarios

Who is the client?

The most fundamental change in the project process to accomplish effective participation is the shift in the interpretation of the word 'client'. The promoter, funder, implementing agency, NGO, all have positions of power in providing the funding and setting out the programme goals. However, the engineer's 'client' is not clear — is it the agency paying for the project or the people using it? By involving men and women, the engineer will be aware of their views. This may lead to a conflict between the programme goals and the wishes of the people. In this case, engineers need to be clear about their position: is the project meeting bottom-up demands or top-down policies? The project team may have to act as intermediaries and speak on behalf of less advantaged members of the community. 'Client' activities, such as project approvals and setting policies have to be negotiated among several stakeholders.

Who manages the service?

There are three main handovers in the conventional project cycle:

- From policy maker to designer,
- From designer to builder and
- From builder to operator.

The last stage is the most difficult. The aims of the design and construction stages may be to produce some technically sound infrastructure, but if the overall aims of the project are to succeed, then the infrastructure needs to be operated and maintained sustainably.

> "While participation of beneficiaries in operation and maintenance is important, project experiences show also that injecting participation for O&M without any earlier consultation does not work. The 'handing over' syndrome characterizes this staged approach to participation: typically, a public work agency constructs a system without conferring with community members, then, just before leaving, the agency informs the community that it is responsible for operation and maintenance. Communities, unless they are in extremely dire straits, have no interest in making the effort to take care of a system they did not ask for and do not own. Experience of project after project confirms this conclusion."

Deepa Narayan

Operation and maintenance may be carried out by a variety of staff, ranging from unskilled volunteers to trained technicians. Only large, financially successful projects will be able to afford the services of a full-time engineer. Even if a municipal engineer is available full or part-time, he or she is likely to have broad rather than specialist training and experience on roads, water supply, buildings and drainage. The policy makers and specialist designers need to be aware that, although they are experts, the operators are likely to have lower levels of technical knowledge and different motivations for carrying out the work. Prospective operators will be better motivated and better prepared if they are involved through the design and construction phases.

Parallel or combined projects?

The management of the delivery of a service may be shared between the promoter and the users, but the users are not a homogenous group. Even when there is a genuine programme goal to involve the users, the degree of gender integration on projects can vary[31], as shown in Figure 4.2.

The first option may be suitable when explicit action will help to balance inequalities or where social (religious or cultural) norms discourage men and women working together. The third approach (sometimes called mainstreaming) may be selected where social issues are not an obstacle to men and women working together, where both men and women have been identified as participants in the project and information can reach men and women equally. The intermediate option may be required if a precedent for shared working has not been set, where women would prefer to work separately, where some capacity development is necessary, or where separate activities would build the confidence of women.

There are advantages and disadvantages with all these options. Separate activities may ensure that men and women's distinctive requirements are clear; women may have more opportunities to make decisions and work outside their traditional roles. However, the activity may still mean that the group is excluded from the benefits of the main part of the project. The activity just focuses on 'women's issues' and is seen as a token activity to fulfil a policy objective. Separate activities to benefit women may also provoke a negative reaction from men, and possibly damage the gender relationship.

---

31. Adapted from *Women and Work*, Susan Bullock. Zed Books Ltd, London, 1994.

The mainstreaming approach increases the excluded group's influence on the core decisions and enables full access to the project's resources (though access to resources may continue to be restricted inadvertently if social barriers are not identified and overcome). It can also be the way to ensure that men accept roles and responsibilities that liberate women for more productive involvement in the infrastructure project.

The intermediate option does ensure access to the resources and gives the socially excluded a clear opportunity to voice their concerns, but again can be seen as a marginal activity.

(a) Some infrastructure or social development projects may be women specific, unrelated to any developments for the wider community

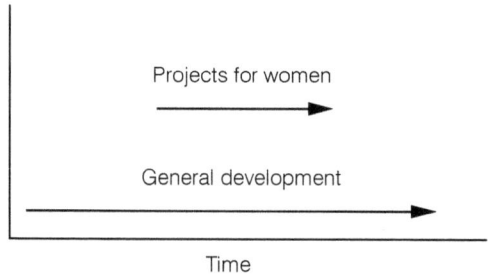

Projects for women

General development

Time

(b) A project component addresses the needs of women but it relates to other work in the community

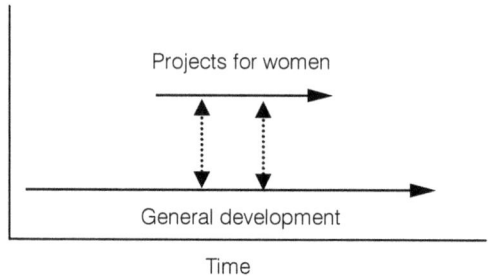

Projects for women

General development

Time

(c) A project may adopt a comprehensive gender approach, with the needs of men and women considered together

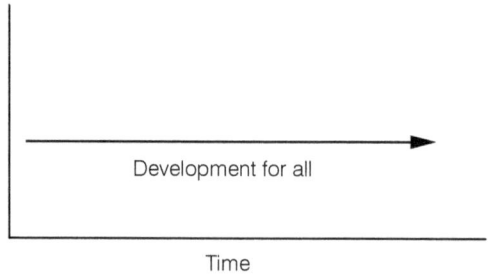

Development for all

Time

Figure 4.2. Projects may target specific groups or address the whole community

A single model is unlikely to be suitable for all activities and an infrastructure project may have to use a mixture of approaches. The activities and education needed to redress social imbalances are likely to benefit from a clear targeting of the disadvantaged, provided they are carried out in the wider context of the project and not treated as an isolated activity. Practical engineering issues are more likely to require a more integrated approach; society can rarely afford separate infrastructure programmes for different groups, so the services provided should meet as wide a range of needs as possible. Narayan (1995) noted that direct technical factors (such as the availability of spare parts) have an impact on participation. People are less likely to get involved if they can see a flaw in the proposals.

Does increasing participation increase equity?

Narayan looked at the relationship of the level of participation on the impact on equitable access to water projects. The data showed only a weak link between the two variables, as high levels of participation may mean that those involved restrict access by others, who have not contributed to the project. Only those who agree to the rules have access, to prevent the problems of free riders taking advantage of other people's work. Of the 121 projects looked at, 65 per cent were rated as having low or medium levels of participation, but 83 per cent had low or medium levels of women's participation*.

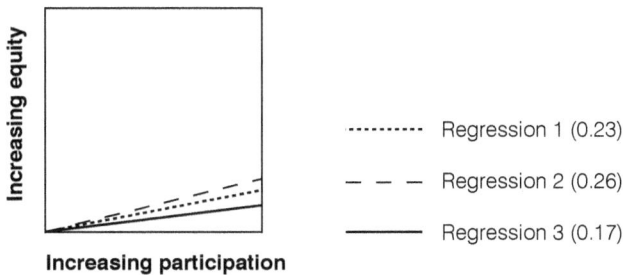

.... Regression 1 (0.23)

— — — Regression 2 (0.26)

———— Regression 3 (0.17)

The Contribution of People's Participation
Evidence from 121 Rural Water supply Projects, Deepa Narayan, World Bank, 1995.

* See the appendix for more information on these graphs. Regression 1 shows the strength of the relation between the two factors. Regression 2 removes the influence of direct factors and regression 3 removes the influence of direct and indirect factors.

Project team

The promoter and the user are important stakeholders; linking the two is the project team. In any engineering project, there is normally a mix of skills, with specialists in technical areas, contracts, management and finance. Like geotechnics or hydrology, participation, especially working with poor women, is a specialist task, so the engineer will have to work with experts where possible to determine the parameters that need to be investigated.

Whilst specialists may be employed to do this, they need to form part of the team, or the benefits of closer involvement of the potential users will be lost. Just as a geotechnical engineer and a structural engineer work together to design foundations, social scientists and engineers need to work together to produce infrastructure that does not exclude people. This requires time to communicate, both among the members of the team and between the team and community. The social scientist will not necessarily be able to explain some of the technical options available, so the engineer is a vital part of the involvement with the community. The costs of employing a social scientist, together with the time the engineer spends discussing the project with the team and the community, need to be included in the budget.

Women engineers

Female engineers are not necessarily better equipped to respond to women's issues than men. They have been through the same technical training as their male colleagues and this technical training does not necessarily provide the socio-economic skills and knowledge required for participative consultations[32]. There will also be a problem if female engineers do not have the same status as their male counterparts. Assigning token female engineers to look at gender can downgrade the status of the social aspects of the project. In circumstances where men have significant social status, the action of senior male project staff coming to meet poor women and listen to their views can have an empowering effect and show that the women's views are important. Female engineers may however have an advantage in that they may be able to attend women's groups or discuss sensitive issues with greater freedom. Within an organization, women may be important in keeping gender on the work agenda.

---

32. In an interview for this research, a female engineer asserted that, as far as her job went, she was the same as her male colleagues, having had the same training and experience.

In some cases, such as cultures where unrelated men and women are not allowed to meet easily, women project staff may be needed to talk to women, but the staff members should have an understanding of the technical issues if these are to be discussed with the community. Similar action may be needed if there is a significant insider/outsider divide between project staff and sectors of the community according to ethnicity, culture, religion or class.

Project programming

The project cycle

Engineers are skilled at programming projects, to ensure that activities are carried out in the correct order and that sufficient time and resources are given to each activity. The project cycle represents a model of the process of planning and implementing projects and programmes. Projects may vary in duration, urgency and scale, but all follow a similar pattern. This sequence is considered here in eight stages[33], though these stages can overlap and sometimes be bypassed or repeated. The specific stages in the project cycle differ between organisations, but the basic concepts are the same. At the end of each stage there will be an output and often a transfer of the lead role in the project. Engineers and managers working with a wide range of development agencies and companies will be familiar with these and able to apply the approach in this chapter to their own situation. Engineers will be most closely involved in the feasibility, design, construction and operation stages, as shown in Figure 4.3, but they also need to be aware how these relate to the rest of the project.

Timing and resources

The cycle is a useful planning model, but engineers regard the infrastructure project process as a linear exercise. The design activity starts with the initial proposals at policy stage and continues through to the construction stage (Figure 4.4).

Activities will overlap – with design decisions being made during the feasibility stage and during construction. Each activity needs to take place in the correct order; the amount and intensity of use of resources will vary from stage to stage. Figure 4.5 shows the project cycle again, but indicates the different durations of the stages (length of arrow) and the amount of

---

33. Based on DFID Guidance Manual on Water Supply and Sanitation Programmes (DFID, 1998) and Civil Engineering Procedure 5th ed (ICE 1996).

resources required (width of arrow). The design and construction stages involve more people and more resources than either the planning stages or the operation. The operation, however, will continue for significantly longer than the involvement of the promoters and engineers, without the same level of inputs and is not seen as a cycle by the users – it has to be sustained. The flow of resources is shown in Figure 4.6, broken down into the capital/construction phase and the operation of the service.

Long-term involvement by users is not restricted to technical issues, such as pump maintenance, or management issues, such as finance collection. Any social action, such as raising the status of women, has to be sustained. Once the project team has completed its stage of the work, the vulnerable in society need to be able to maintain any improvements to their social status. Projects therefore need to plan the operation and maintenance

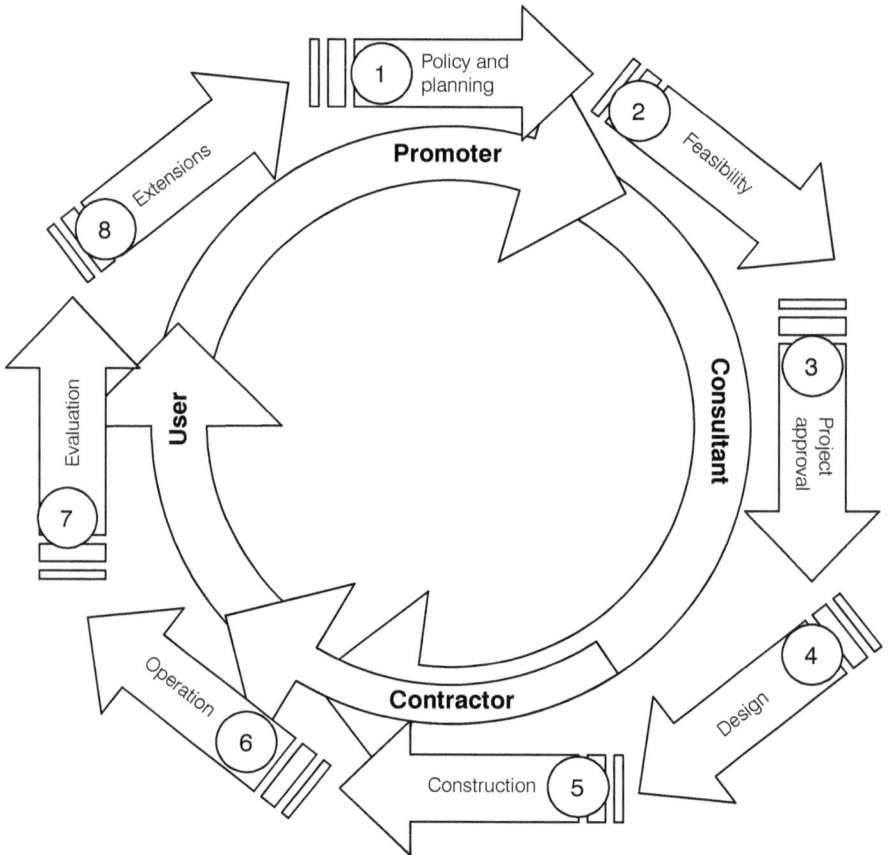

Figure 4.3. A project cycle and main participants

and the social development activities to be sustained with the resources available.

The project stage length and resources will vary from project to project. For example, a capital-intensive road project will have more resources during the construction stage than a sanitation promotion project, which may concentrate its resources in planning and monitoring.

The project stages give an impression of discrete activities. This may be true for the policy maker handing over the project to a consultant then to a contractor and then to the management, but to the community the process is continuous. Staging projects or phasing implementation may be a useful management process, but participants must be involved in these handovers, so the process is understood and momentum is not lost.

The indications of timing and resources in the second project cycle diagram are for a 'conventional' project. The balance would change to suit the project. For example, emergency responses have short development periods, with planning and design occurring in a matter of days. The operating costs of a sewerage scheme will be much greater than the resources required to manage on-plot sanitation. Other changes may be required to meet the requirements of a wider group of stakeholders. When women or other socially excluded groups are included in the design and

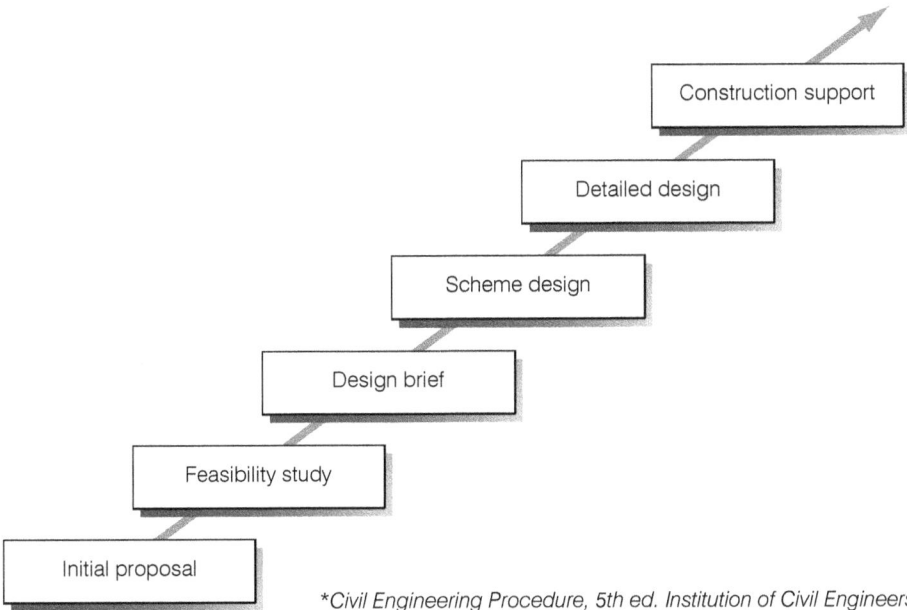

Construction support

Detailed design

Scheme design

Design brief

Feasibility study

Initial proposal

Civil Engineering Procedure, 5th ed. Institution of Civil Engineers.

Figure 4.4. Stages in the development of project design*

Flexible timescale for a water supply project

Peasant women in Dodata sub district, Ethiopia, who spent 4 - 6 hours each day fetching water identified lack of easy access to clean water as their main problem. From the beginning there was no project blue print and no time schedule to follow, so allowing many people to influence the shape and content of the project. Women were trained to operate and maintain the communal water points, and to manage the overall scheme e.g. keep the books and collect fees. There was continuous dialogue between the women and the technical designer of the project, which led to some innovative adaptations of the standard design. This was one of the factors leading to a strong sense of ownership of the project. The project took six years from identification to its handing over to the local community.

Evaluation Synthesis of Rural Water Supply Projects,
Evaluation Report no. 596, DFID, May 1997, p.26

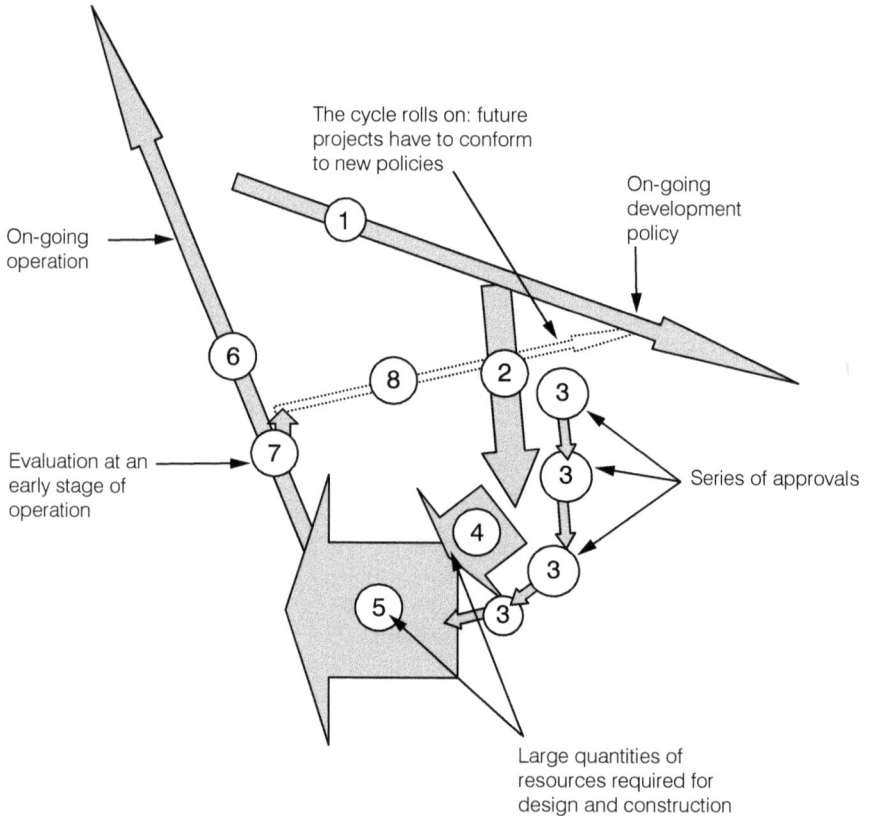

Figure 4.5. Length and cost of project stages

construction process, this will take additional time. This is not just due to the actual time of consultation meetings, but the fact that the meetings may only be held when women have spare time to attend a meeting. This may be outside harvest periods, or only in the evening when they have finished their other tasks. Men tend to be able to plan their time more flexibly, as they do not have the same number of demands from their children or the sick to consider.

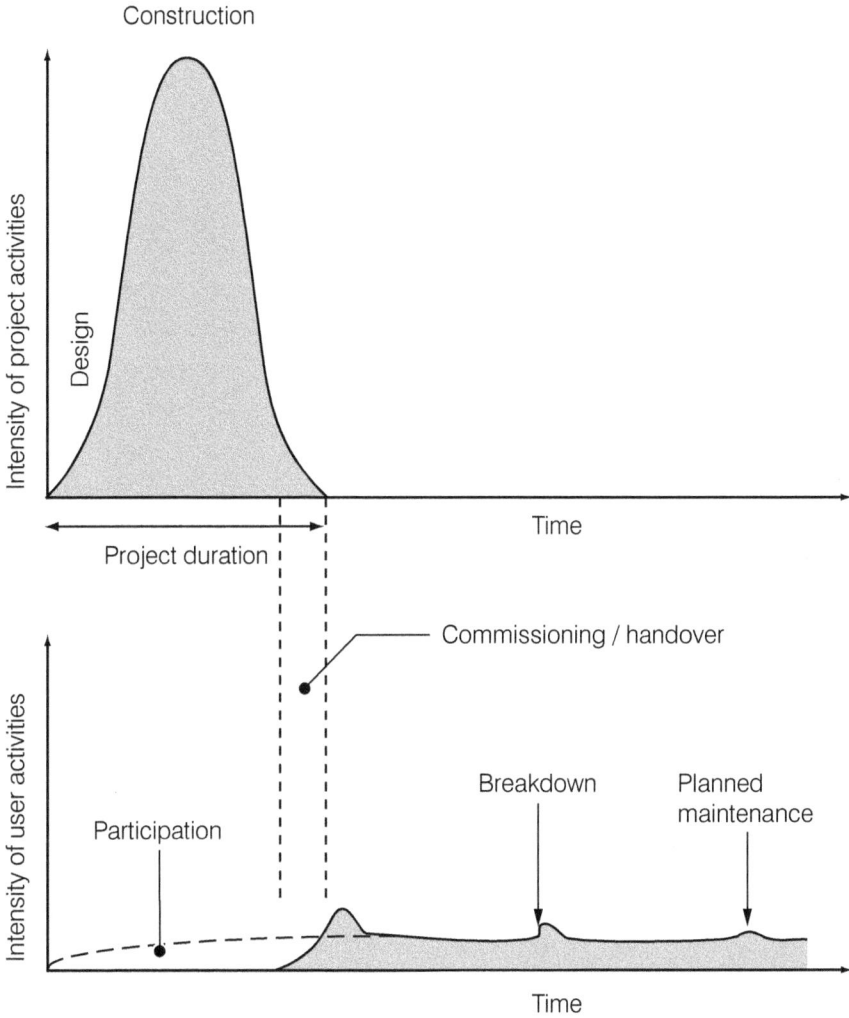

Figure 4.6. Project programme and resources

Malawi gravity flow schemes

In 1968, the Community Development and Social Welfare Department began to support the self-help construction of schools and other community buildings. Water was identified as an issue (**policy**). After two pilot schemes (**feasibility**), a scheme for 75,000 people was started (**design and construction**). The operational procedures were developed over two years and the scheme has been providing water, to a greater or lesser extent, for up to thirty years (**operation**). A World Bank/WHO study was carried out three years after construction (**evaluation**). Additional projects were started elsewhere before the construction had been completed (**project extensions**).

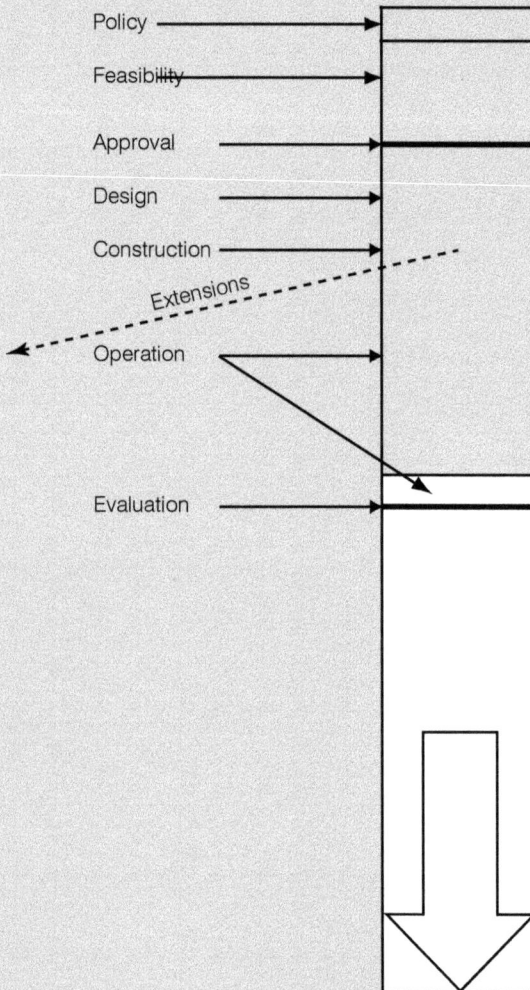

Policy

Feasibility

Approval

Design

Construction

Extensions

Operation

Evaluation

Village water supply in the Decade – Lessons from field experience.
C Glennie, Wiley, Chichester, 1983

Planning for participation

The conventional project stages are a useful planning tool, but they may not be so clear from a community perspective and they may break continuity in the project. Stakeholder involvement throughout the cycle will also go through several stages, as shown in Figure 4.7:

- representation in policy formulation;
- training, capacity building, information sharing;
- participation in delivering the project;
- management of the facilities; and
- more representation, progressively increasing the voice of the socially excluded.

The stages in the involvement of men and women in the project have to be integrated into the project cycle.

> *"Participation should be viewed as a process that starts with planning and ends with operation and maintenance, rather than as an element that can be injected in the later stages of a project whenever outsiders determine. Effective participation takes many forms – there is no one ideal form."*
>
> Deepa Narayan

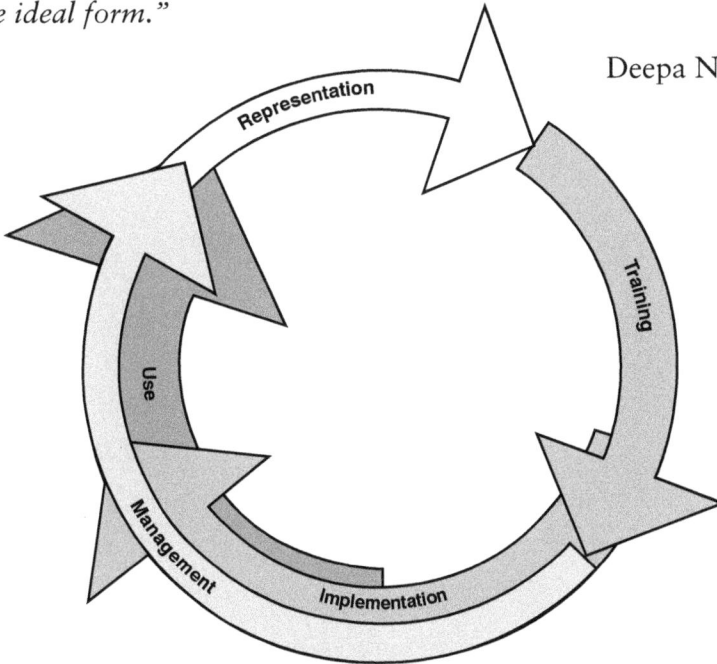

Figure 4.7. Participation in the project cycle

Does increasing participation improve implementation?

Narayan found that overall beneficiary participation was the critical determinant of overall quality of implementation. Other important factors in the quality of implementation were clarity of objectives and availability of spare parts and technicians.

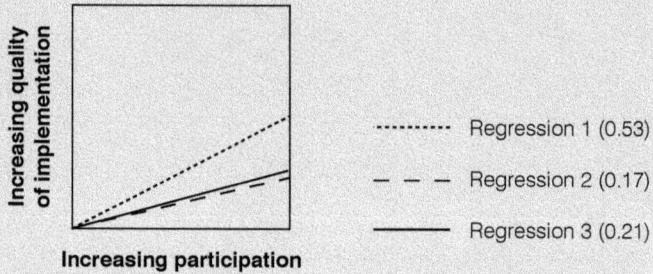

Increasing quality of implementation

Increasing participation

·········· Regression 1 (0.53)

– – – Regression 2 (0.17)

———— Regression 3 (0.21)

Source: *The Contribution of People's Participation – Evidence from 121 Rural Water supply Projects,* Deepa Narayan, World Bank, 1995*

*For an explanation of this research, see the appendix.

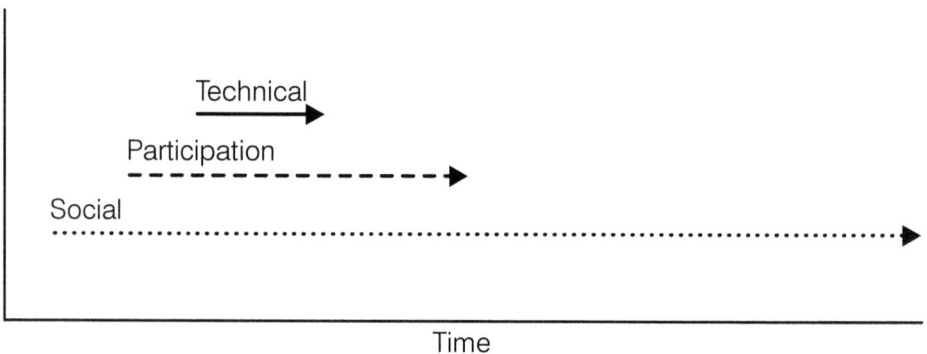

Technical

Participation

Social

Time

Figure 4.8. Project timescales

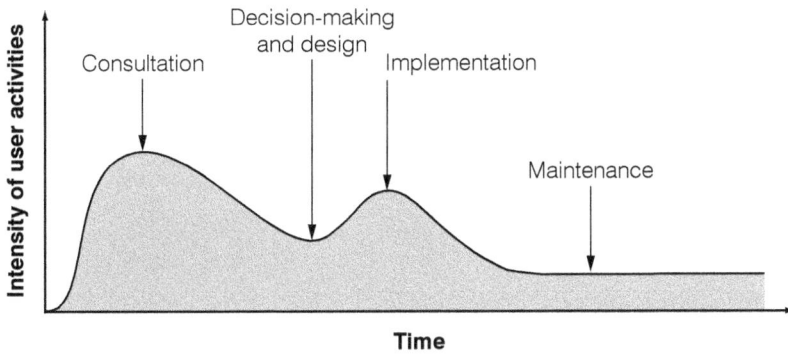

Figure 4.9. Patterns of participation

Participation does take time and money and so should be scheduled and budgeted to start alongside other investigations, such as geotechnical surveys and hydrological measurements.

The time scales for participation in different aspects of the project are unlikely to match technical requirements. A water project that could be technically planned and implemented in a year may have to be spread over several years to allow full participation, as the community may not be able to afford the time and inputs necessary in such a short period. If gender aspects are going to be fully integrated, the process may take even longer, as the socially excluded need to be supported through skills and confidence building before they can enter into a meaningful dialogue. After the project has finished, the work on social inclusion still needs to continue (Figure 4.8).

Participation can also vary during the cycle. Guijt[34] noted that consultation and construction had a high level of participation, but the main decision-making phase was still exclusive (Figure 4.9). She notes that 100 per cent participation is a myth and intensities and forms of participation should be assessed in the local context.

Impacts on project programming

Just using participative methods will not ensure the involvement of poor men and women. Active steps have to be taken to overcome the social

34. *Myth of Community,* eds. Guijt and Shah, ITDG, UK, 1998.

Narayan looked at the relationship of the level of participation and other outcomes of water supply projects. Involving people in decision-making led to increased initiative, leadership and confidence in the community. Participation did not bypass local leadership, but had a positive effect on them. The full multivariate coefficients are shown.

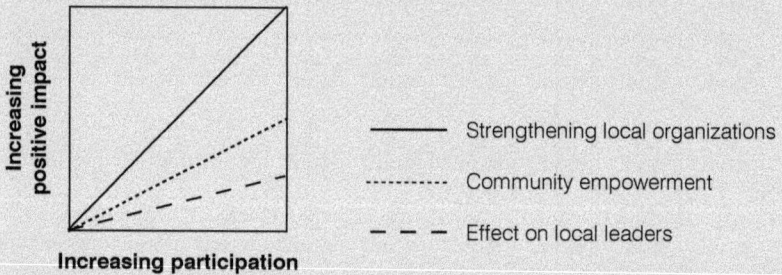

Increasing positive impact (y-axis)

Increasing participation (x-axis)

——— Strengthening local organizations

·········· Community empowerment

– – – Effect on local leaders

Note that this data is for communities and does not necessarily reflect the involvement of marginalized groups.

The Contribution of People's Participation – Evidence from 121 Rural Water supply Projects, Deepa Narayan, World Bank, 1995

barriers that contribute to their exclusion, and these need to be included in the project programme. Steps include:

• Being aware of the issue — do only men turn up to meetings? Do some people never speak in meetings? Consider who is addressed during site visits.

• Adopting an iterative approach to identifying and responding to social exclusion – do the female participants represent women in general, or just those living nearby with time to spare? Are the men (or women) at meetings the rich or the unemployed?

• Having meetings when men and women can attend — this may involve separate meetings, but different sectors of society do have to hear and accept others' views and priorities.

• Holding meetings in a way that men and women, articulate and silent, literate and illiterate have opportunities to make their voice and choice heard – this may involve separate meetings.

- Where separate meetings are held (men or women, national or local government, specialists or range of stakeholders), the information and viewpoints of each group need to be fed back to the other stakeholders.
- Tailoring the information presented and the questions asked to the technical capabilities of the different social groups.
- Identifying indicators and monitoring them as the project progresses.
- Providing additional training or discussion time with less advantaged groups.
- Ensuring that representatives are representative. Can educated women provide a better insight into the lives of poor women than traditional male leaders who have complex links with all levels of the community?
- Maintaining an awareness of social exclusion and the problems of assumptions and stereotypes with the project team. Too great a concentration on one social group may lead to the exclusion of others. If hygiene is just promoted to women, will men get the message?

There is no blueprint for participation; experienced, well-resourced staff are needed to ensure that the project addresses the local situation. Required resources include time, budgets and a commitment from the project promoter.

The costs of participation

Involving men and women may be efficient in terms of the overall objectives of the project, but to be successful it does require time and money – both for the project team and for the local people giving up their time to contribute. The costs and benefits of participation are financial, social and psychological. Clients and communities will only participate effectively when benefits are greater than the costs. Examples of activities that need to be included in any project budgets and programmes include:

- consultation/participation activities, including the project staff needed to run them;
- overtime for staff, as meetings may have to be held when it is convenient for community groups, e.g. in the evening;
- travel costs to meet community groups;
- recruiting female engineers and technicians to work with women's groups, as it may not be acceptable for men to meet with women in certain areas;

- investigating and designing several options to enable people to choose appropriate technologies;
- providing additional training to women in the community who are to be employed on the scheme. Women often have not received the same level of education as men and so, in addition to the technical training provided by the project, they may require support and simplified systems that do not depend on literacy or numeracy skills;
- matching the programme to meet the community's pace of development, rather than carrying out the work in the shortest possible time; and
- increasing uncertainty in each project stage.

What is the cost?

A group of water users in Rwanda who managed their own system changed rules when they discovered that women were spending as much time collecting fees as they had earlier spent collecting water.

Yacoob and Walker, 1991, quoted in Narayan, 1995

Participation may imply an involvement by the community, but it can still ignore the needs of socially and economically disadvantaged groups.

"Attitudes and behaviours which are dominating and discriminatory are common amongst those of us who are men: to become aware of these is a first and often difficult step. Even when the application of participatory methodologies is intended to minimize biases, women are often marginalized. Again and again, women are excluded by factors like time and place of meeting, composition of groups, conventions that only men speak in public, outsiders being only or mainly men, and men talking to men. In communities, it's easier for men than women to find the undisturbed blocks of time needed for [participatory] mapping, diagramming, discussions and analysis. The best times for women to meet, sometimes late after dark, are often inconvenient for outsiders. When outsiders rush, make short visits, do not stay the night, and come only once or twice, it is typically difficult for local women to participate, and issues of gender are likely to be marginalized or excluded. ...Recognizing and offsetting these biases requires sensitivity, patience and commitment on the part of those who are outsiders to a community."

Robert Chambers in The Myth of Community, Gujit and Shah, 1998

The following chapters look at engineers' work from three different viewpoints.

Chapter 5 examines how social inclusion can be fostered through the project cycle.

Chapter 6 gives an introduction into how technology can have a social impact on communities, looking at various sectors in turn.

Chapter 7 encourages engineers to look at their own organization, to ensure that institutions can be as inclusive as the infrastructure and services they provide.

5

From foundations to finish

The engineer's involvement changes from stage to stage as projects progress. For enlightened engineers seeking to contribute to social equity as well as meeting a design brief, opportunities for promoting inclusive participation arise in different ways in each stage. International guidelines on sustainable development, national policies on gender and poverty reduction, Millennium Development Goals and comparative case studies can all be called upon to justify measures to foster maximum participation of all stakeholders.

In Chapter 5, we look at the project cycle for infrastructure projects in more detail and the many potential entry points for enhancing the involvement of women, the poor, and socially disadvantaged groups. Key points are:

- Existing national and international guidelines should influence Terms of Reference and Project Briefs – implicitly and explicitly.
- Feasibility studies offer an early opportunity for the wishes of local men and women to be investigated.
- Inclusive participation is an engineering 'factor of safety' to reduce the risk of a sustainability failure, but it has significant time and resource impacts that have to be agreed with client(s), donors, promoters and user groups from the start.
- Outline designs and standards need to be flexible and may need to be adapted to reflect the inputs of different user groups.
- Women can be involved in all stages including construction, but may need training and appropriate working conditions.
- Operation and maintenance can be planned and designed to make the tasks open to all sectors of society.
- Monitoring and evaluation needs to be participatory too, and the indicators used should measure social impacts as well as engineering outputs.

As projects progress, the type of work an engineer carries out changes, from planning to design to construction. Each stage is determined by outputs from preceding work, so an understanding of how policy influences design and how construction influences operation helps to put each phase of the project in context. Ways of addressing inequalities in society also vary with each project stage. Narayan (1995) found that including people throughout the project cycle had significantly more impact than just including participation in a single stage.

Policy and planning

This initial stage is also known as policy development, sector planning or programme formulation. Issues such as poverty reduction, health improvements, the status of women and economic development are explored and targets then set. International, national, state or local public organisations, private companies and non-governmental organisations (NGOs) may be involved in developing plans, either as 'clients', donors or advisers. Engineers within these organisations need to look beyond technical issues and encourage participatory planning and policy development wherever possible. As engineers work to implement these policies, they have a role both in interpreting the policy to suit the local situation and providing feedback to ensure that policies reflect reality.

International guidelines

International guidelines can determine which projects get funding and influence how they are carried out. They provide a framework and guidance on internationally accepted practice. Knowledge of globally endorsed principles like the Dublin principles and guidelines on sustainable development or gender equity emerging from international conferences equips the engineer to seek to influence the Terms of Reference (TOR) or Project Brief in an authoritative way[35].

National policies and plans

Policies at national level may take the form of explicit goals or may be implicit from the legal system. They may be influenced by international policies and national priorities, shaped by political lobbying and research findings. Participation by men and women at this level is through the political process. However, women have less than ten percent of parliamentary seats in all areas of the world, apart from East Asia and the

---

35. *Implementing Labour Standards in Construction — a Sourcebook* (Ladbury, Cotton and Jennings, WEDC, 2003), has examples of contract clauses to comply with international labour standards.

Pacific[36], so measures are required to include their views using alternative channels.

National Plans and Poverty Reduction Strategy Papers (PRSPs) set priorities, targets and planned investments. The agreed process for preparation of PRSPs includes consultation with civic society, which may be a possible route for the voices of socially disadvantaged groups to be heard.

Programme policies

Government departments, NGOs and individual programmes will normally have their own specific policies and these may include specific requirements on gender equity and participatory processes. If so, it is important to check that they are supported with the necessary resources. Narayan (1995) found that only 17 per cent of the projects investigated in her study had a high level of participation of women, despite the fact that most projects identified them as a target group.

Vertical integration

National policies set the agenda for programmes and should feed into the project Terms of Reference (TOR), Memorandum of Understanding, Project Brief or logical framework. Policies should be accompanied by the appropriate resources to implement the plans. Omitting participation and gender activities from the TOR may make it difficult to include them at a later date and secure the necessary resources. Even if they are added later in the project cycle, they will be "bolted on" to the project and not integrated with the rest of the activities. Engineers will need to understand the policy objectives included in TORs and address them in their tenders. Where TORs restrict or are silent about participatory approaches, it may be appropriate to seek clarification and to make clear that the engineer's working methods will seek to incorporate international guidelines and national policies on gender or social development into the different project stages.

> "Beneficiary participation in decision-making was ... important in achieving effective operation and maintenance, but such participation implies that agencies must let go of decision-making at the micro-level. Agencies, especially government engineering departments, have found this particularly difficult to accomplish."

> Deepa Narayan

---

36. Engendering Development Through Gender Equality in *Rights, Resources, and Voice*, Oxford University Press, World Bank, 2001

Dublin Principles

At the International Conference on Water and the Environment in Dublin, Ireland, in 1992, expert representatives from a hundred countries adopted the following principles.

Principle No. 1
Fresh water is a finite and vulnerable resource, essential to sustain life, development and the environment

Since water sustains life, effective management of water resources demands a holistic approach, linking social and economic development with protection of natural ecosystems. Effective management links land and water uses across the whole of a catchment area or groundwater aquifer.

Principle No. 2
Water development and management should be based on a participatory approach, involving users, planners and policy-makers at all levels

The participatory approach involves raising awareness of the importance of water among policy-makers and the general public. It means that decisions are taken at the lowest appropriate level, with full public consultation and involvement of users in the planning and implementation of water projects.

Principle No. 3
Women play a central part in the provision, management and safe-guarding of water

This pivotal role of women as providers and users of water and guardians of the living environment has seldom been reflected in institutional arrangements for the development and management of water resources. Acceptance and implementation of this principle requires positive policies to address women's specific needs and to equip and empower women to participate at all levels in water resources programmes, including decision-making and implementation, in ways defined by them.

Principle No. 4
Water has an economic value in all its competing uses and should be recognised as an economic good

Within this principle, it is vital to recognise first the basic right of all human beings to have access to clean water and sanitation at an affordable price. Past failure to recognise the economic value of water has led to wasteful and environmentally damaging uses of the resource. Managing water as an economic good is an important way of achieving efficient and equitable use, and of encouraging conservation and protection of water resources.

"Participation is necessary to ensure that conflicting interests are harmonized and that inequities are removed. Communities and individuals that are underserved — including the urban poor and the socially excluded, such as ethnic minorities and indigenous peoples – need to be mainstreamed; ADB will promote the recentering of such communities and individuals. Given the essential nature of private sector participation, without which there will be little infusion of capital and expertise, and of much needed technology, ADB will seek to draw private enterprise into participating in a higher quality of water service provision. Simultaneously, ADB recognizes that women are important water users, clients, and beneficiaries, as well as managers of water for family nutrition, hygiene, health, and community activities. Equally, women are development agents, professionals, and decision-makers in water sector activities. ADB will strengthen women's ability to participate more effectively through discrete programs targeted at educating women, empowering them, and enabling their involvement in community-based decision making. Water projects supported by ADB will incorporate carefully designed components that promote the participation of civil society in identifying needs and issues, designing solutions, and establishing mechanisms for monitoring and dispute resolution."

The Water Policy of the Asian Development Bank

Policy for equity and efficiency

"...the full participation of both men and women in all Red Cross and Red Crescent actions not only ensures gender equality, but also increases the efficiency and effectiveness of the work of the organization;"

from the International Federation of Red Cross
and Red Crescent Societies Gender Policy

To ensure polices are put into practice, indicators need to established at this stage to measure impact and effectiveness at each stage of the project; it is too late if indicators are only identified and measured during project evaluation.

Horizontal integration

Policies do not only need to filter down to the project level, they also need to be integrated between ministries and sectors if inconsistencies are not to create problems. A national gender policy may not be referred to in a water policy and vice versa, but they are both agreed statements influencing the development process. The language and actions identified may vary and even conflict between policies.

Engineers, project managers and technicians do not need a policy mandate to include cost effectiveness, safety or durability in their designs or construction techniques as it is part of their professional duty. Working with local men and women in developing and managing infrastructure is becoming a standard method of working in low-income countries that engineers should adopt without being specifically instructed to do. They do however need to state explicitly what form social inclusion is going to take, to demonstrate conformity with social polices.

Lobbying

A conventional project is a top-down process, with the impetus for the development being initiated, funded and directed to meet policy goals. The engineer acts as an intermediary, translating policy goals into action. Information also needs to flow in the other direction, as the demands and priorities of the users will need to be fed back to the policy makers, so they can continuously adjust their actions. Other intermediaries, such as local government or politicians, do not have the infrastructure expertise to liase between the two groups on technical issues.

Feasibility

The second stage of the project cycle (feasibility) moves from the national level to the local level, from the general to the specific. The feasibility stage of programmes examines projects that can put into practice the promoter's plans, moving from policy to product. In emergencies, this stage may be significantly reduced, but under normal circumstances it is a vital way to test out what will and will not work. Some of the discussion and consultations will be at national level, but it is also important to start a dialogue with men and women at the local level. Feasibility studies look at various options (such as alternative routes for a pipeline), and rank them on their viability. The detail required by the study will depend on how well developed the promoter's plans are. A series of studies may be required, for example to support a plan for improved transport, then select the route and then choose procurement strategies. Feasibility studies may be repeated and refined to reduce uncertainty. It is important to select the correct project early in the cycle, as the cost of changes increases as the project progresses (see Figure 5.1). Leaving participation to a later stage of the project deprives the users of significant choices and is likely to entail increased costs, as work may have to be repeated.

Costs and benefits

In the feasibility stage, different options are ranked against the programme objectives. In commercial projects this may be a simple rate of return comparison on the capital invested, looking at the net present value of each option. These valuations have to consider the whole life of the scheme, from design to decommissioning and replacement and take account of the uncertainties at each stage. The time scale involved will vary, with uncertainty increasing for longer projections. In development projects, however, the objectives will not only be the immediate financial returns but economic returns at a wider level, such as contributions to the national or local economy and fulfilling other policy criteria.

Engineers are trained to balance competing demands, such as quality of materials versus cost, safety versus speed of construction. These factors can be weighted to adjust each cost or benefit according to the programme priorities. Thus a project that has greater positive impact on the lives of poor women may be given a higher priority than a project that has a greater cash return on the investment. This has to be included in the project objectives however, as otherwise it may be difficult to prioritise aiming for social gains that are difficult to quantify as against achieving simple economic impacts.

Cost benefit analysis should also identify *who* pays the costs and *who* reaps the benefit. A hydroelectric dam that is planned without taking into account the views of local inhabitants may produce positive benefits overall, but the benefits may only be acquired by a minority of industrialists with the costs being borne by those adversely affected by the development. Large investments are often political issues with lobbying by special interest groups. The feasibility study is one way for the opinions of those people normally excluded from the political system to be heard.

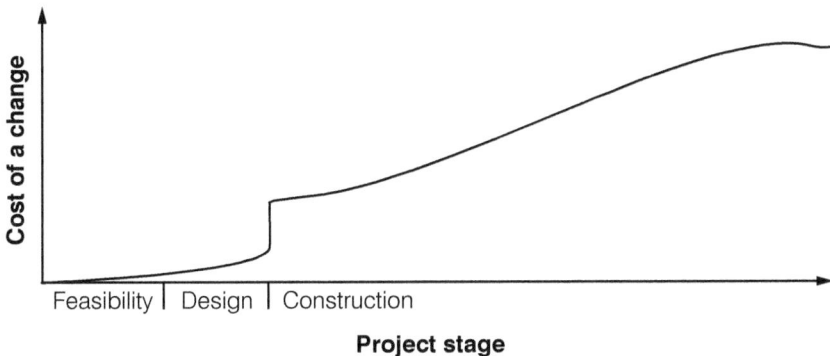

*From *Civil Engineering Procedure,* 5th ed., ICE, 1996.

Figure 5.1. Cost of change against project stage*

81

"During a project identification assignment for DFID in Guyana, some remote Amerindian communities (accessible only by plane) were visited and their needs and priorities were discussed at community meetings attended by both women and men. It became clear that the priority for women was water since they had to walk some miles to a spring. The men however were adamant that the priority for a development must be construction of a road in order to increase the opportunity for income generating activities. During the meetings, no consensus could be reached on these differing perspectives."

Sarah Parry-Jones, Consultant

Collecting data for project planning

Engineers always need data to plan and design infrastructure. Feasibility studies have to balance the detail of the data with the effort spent obtaining it. Data collected should be timely, sufficient, accurate and specific. A large-scale census may not detail issues such as gender roles. Targeted separate interviews with men and women and direct observation can give a clearer view of their condition and position in society.

Some data may be readily available from secondary sources like government ministries, other projects, NGOs or donor agencies. At the feasibility stage though there is nearly always a need for specific data to be collected. Engineers will normally undertake site visits to gather site information such as topography, soil type, existing levels of service, consumption patterns

Willingness-to-pay studies from three continents

A 1987-1990 World Bank funded survey into the demand for water in rural areas of Latin America, South Asia and Africa recognised gender differences in preferences regarding water supply as well as in access to and control over finances. Variations in willingness-to-pay were partly explained by the sex of the respondent, though not in a consistent direction. In Tanzania and Haiti women appeared willing to pay considerably more than men for access to public taps. However in Nigeria and India they were not prepared to pay as much. Despite women's positive response to the suggestion of improved water supplies, they were reluctant to commit the household to a substantial financial contribution — perhaps because they had limited influence over household finances.

World Bank Water Demand Research Team, 1993

and potential sources for a water supply project. When the population, water consumption, crops grown, travel patterns or other parameters are determined, the numbers relating to men and women should be recorded separately (disaggregated). This is required to understand the differing roles, needs and priorities that men and women have within a community.

Obtaining socio-economic data cannot just be achieved by looking at census or survey data. Gathering subjective or qualitative data, such as where people want a bus stop or where latrines should be sited, needs to be carried out in the correct way. Meteorologists have very specific ways of measuring rainfall; measuring people's opinions needs a similar rigour. Social scientists have developed techniques to provide useful data. Some of these methods require the investigator to discuss the issues with all sectors of the community, rather than remaining a remote observer. The skills involved in establishing people's preferences, beliefs, practices and opinions will require the engineer to work with social scientists, both in developing the issues to be investigated and responding to the results.

Determining what is local culture to be respected and what is social inequality to be challenged is a difficult decision and can be influenced by preconceptions, lack of awareness, pressure from powerful groups and external factors. Even when a group of people is clearly disadvantaged, the level of response has to relate to the willingness of the community to address the issue and the resources, expertise and time the development team can provide to support any action. It is important not to leave the vulnerable group in a worse position due to short-term, externally driven reactions.

Feedback

The feasibility report is an opportunity for the project team to feed back information from all parties involved. Thus, if issues such as the participation of women have not been included in the terms of reference, evidence that this is required can be included in the feasibility report. At this stage, the project team will have a greater knowledge of the issues than the planners had when they were drawing up the policy and Terms of Reference.

Project selection and approval

Project selection and approval criteria need to be developed with care to encompass the ways in which social and gender aspects are to be included in the project. These then set the framework for the detailed decisions.

The project will have to go through various approval stages. The funding body will need to appraise and approve the planned project after the feasibility stage. A second appraisal may take place towards the end of the design stage to approve the project before any contracts are prepared and let.

The project documents will be reviewed to see if they match the original plans and policies. Major issues that will be considered will include costs and time scales, but there will also be policies on participation, gender or sustainability. The people appraising the project will want proof that the scheme will produce the planned outputs. Social inclusion can be considered alongside more concrete issues, such as technical feasibility and economic impact. For example, a project based in an area with a high proportion of female-headed households may have a greater development impact than an alternative project with a higher cash return on the investment. If engineers and project managers want to increase the likelihood of a project being approved, they should ensure that all the policy issues are clearly addressed in the reports and other project outputs.

Approval by the funding body is only half of the approval stage. Agreement and acceptance by the community also has to be considered.

Design

Design brief

Preparation of an outline design may be part of the feasibility study, planning approval or bidding process. Promoters will need to see concrete ideas in order to compare options. In a competitive tendering process, the engineer will have to bid for the design work based on a brief. In order to gain an advantage over other companies, the tender should show that the designer understands how the infrastructure development fits in with the

In Shinyanga Region, Tanzania, the water project uses a participative exercise with men and women in a general meeting to assess current practices and preferences on water sources.

- Different pictures showing different types of water sources that are present in the village are displayed together with other types found in neighbouring villages or towns.
- An envelope is placed under every type of water source.
- Every person present is given a small piece of plain paper with a different colour for women and men.
- The people are then asked to vote for the water source they presently use by placing the piece of paper in the envelope under their choice. Everybody does this freely, it is easy for the women because they are not required to speak aloud.
- The results are counted separately for men and women and recorded aside.
- Then they are asked to vote again for the type of water source they would like to have, and the same process of counting repeats.

Consolata Sana, Tanzania, in *Working with Women and Men on Water and Sanitation*, Occasional Paper 25, IRC

promoter's overall plans and policies. Ensuring that policies, such as the inclusion of women in the project, are addressed will add to the strength of the bid.

Feasibility studies, planning approvals or bidding processes do not necessarily permit consultation with the community during preparation of the outline design, due to lack of time, resources, commercial confidentiality or to limit community expectations. Designers should be aware of these constraints and regard any outline design as a means of initiating dialogue with the community, to be adapted and revised as necessary, rather than a plan that only needs the detail adding. It is easier to change an outline design at this early stage than to add mitigation measures later on. Statutory or donor approval of a design should not be used as an excuse for not altering the plans to suit the needs of people unable to influence polices and projects at an earlier stage. A short delay in resubmitting revised plans is to be preferred to building infrastructure that does not meet the needs of the people who are meant to benefit from it.

Data collection

Engineers will be familiar with the need to collect data to support the design. Much of the initial work will have been carried out during the feasibility stage, but further detail will be required. This is the first stage where local people, as opposed to their representatives, can be closely involved. Men and women do not only need to be consulted about socio-economic data, or where they would like roads, water points or markets to be sited, but can contribute to specifically technical matters. This flow of data is two-way, as the design stage allows a dialogue to develop with all social groups, with the engineer explaining possible options and listening to the comments of various groups within the community. The potential development should be balanced by a realisation that there are limits and costs involved. Expectations that all needs will be addressed should not be raised or disappointment may damage the final outcome.

Scheme design

The technical design of the project is only one part of the designer's duties. Before detailed design is started, the engineer will need to look at a variety of issues, such as costs, that relate to the whole life of the scheme, including;

- construction;
- commissioning;
- operation and maintenance;
- future additions or changes in use; and
- decommissioning.

It is preferable to consult with the organisation that will be responsible for each of these subsequent activities. In conventional projects, the contractors, operating staff and promoters can be asked to give their views. In a community-managed scheme, many of these tasks will be carried out by the community and so they should be consulted. In a conventional scheme, the design engineers can send plans and specifications to colleagues for their comments. In community-managed schemes, the engineer will have to explain the implications of the scheme design and any alternative options, in order that the comments received are informed and relevant. Different groups within the community may be responsible for different aspects of the whole life of the scheme. A 'representative' body should be consulted, but more detailed work may be needed to reach, say, the women who will be paying for water or the artisans who will be maintaining a road.

"In a water supply project, an engineer was investigating sources of local building materials. Stone was quarried locally, with men digging out the stone and women breaking it into smaller pieces by hand. The engineer could adapt the design to suit these local supplies, rather than insisting on standard aggregate that could only be sourced from outside the area, with obvious implications for the cost and sustainability of the project. Using the local supply would also provide employment for the men and women in the quarry, and increase the benefits of the project to the local economy."

Brian Reed, WEDC

Does increasing participation improve design?

Narayan was puzzled by the lack of strength in the relationship between the quality of design and beneficiary participation. Further analysis of the data showed that 'beneficiary participation' did not just include users, but also government staff and other stakeholders with less of a stake in the details of the design. Only 6 out of the 121 projects examined actually had direct participation in the design of the systems. Other projects used indirect information (market surveys, contingent valuations etc.), which though contributing to the quality of the design, was not considered participative.

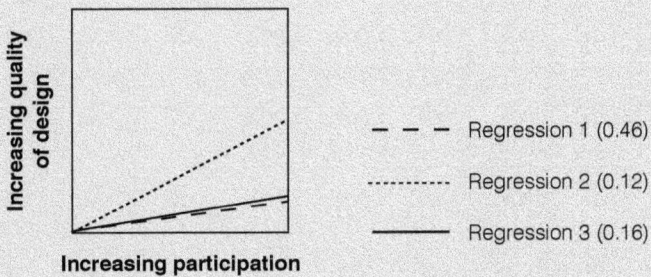

Regression 1 (0.46)

Regression 2 (0.12)

Regression 3 (0.16)

The Contribution of People's Participation – Evidence from 121 Rural Water supply Projects, Deepa Narayan, World Bank, 1995[†]

Detailed design

Design is a specialist task, which is why engineers with many years training and experience are needed for the task. Some of the technical decisions may be 'gender neutral' and the community does not need to be consulted. There may be fewer neutral decisions than is at first apparent and, anyway, the benefits of developing community ownership mean that as many decisions as possible should be shared ones.

Standardization and choice

The use of standard components does make design, construction and replacement of the infrastructure cheaper and faster. However, a single inappropriate technology will negate any savings made. Finding out what solution is appropriate (not necessarily the 'best') can be achieved in a variety of ways:

- observation — see how men and women currently carry out tasks, such as washing or collecting water;
- discussion, asking them what are important design features;
- presentation of a variety of options to choose from, in a way that the local men and women can understand — for example demonstration models — not engineering drawings;
- developing designs with the community (e.g. making models or prototypes); or
- training men and women to develop their own ideas and build them (e.g. sanplats, washing slabs).

For more details about making the design process more user-friendly, see *Designing water supply and sanitation projects to meet demand, Books 1-3*, WEDC, 2002.

Construction support

The design process does not stop with the production of the final drawings and specification. The designer needs to be involved during the construction stage to answer queries and change the design when preferable solutions become apparent. It is often only during construction that people can appreciate the design and then suggest improvements and adaptations to suit their needs. The informal situation of a building site may allow people to voice their concerns, as opposed to the formal atmosphere of a public meeting.

Construction

The construction stage of a project involves the greatest amount of investment of resources. It is also when many people can be involved in the project. It is the most public phase of the engineering process.[37]

Procurement strategies

The project may be implemented in various ways including by:

- formal construction contracts, such as:
  - a traditional design by a consulting engineer or government staff and construction by a contractor or direct labour;
  - a design and build scheme — either directly by the promoter's staff or contracted out;
  - a build, own, operate and transfer concession (BOOT); or
- informal contracts, such as:
  - a community approach, with voluntary labour, in-kind contributions and food for work schemes;
  - self-help, with the community being provided training and resources to carry out the work themselves.

Where formal contracts are used, many of the social benefits that could be realised are left out because the engineer drafting the contract is not aware of them or does not think they are suitable activities to be included in the specification. Traditional contractors (managed by engineers) will not be working in a team with social scientists. They may not realise what positive or negative impact they can have on the project through their work practices and may have no mandate to use more socially inclusive construction methods.

The construction method selected will depend on many issues. Engineering issues include contractual arrangements, construction programming, quality control and cost. Social issues include employment opportunities, gaining skills and experience, taking part in the construction to feel that the project is 'owned' locally, gaining confidence and status within the community. However these social considerations are often overlooked, because social scientists may not realise that people can be involved in construction whilst engineers may not be aware of the wider, long-term benefits of such an action. There are many opportunities to involve men and women in the project at this stage.

---

37. *Implementing Labour Standards in Construction* – a sourcebook (Ladbury, Cotton and Jennings), WEDC 2003 has practical guidance on social aspects of construction.

Whatever method is selected, the involvement of men and women will depend on the awareness and skills of the personnel involved and the performance criteria and payment indicators selected. The size, budget and sequence of each stage can impact on people's involvement, especially if social and technical tasks are separated or carried out in the wrong order.

Payment

Contracts specify various indicators that are used to pay for the work. This may be for cubic metre of excavation, metre length of trench, time spent digging or on completion of the whole trench. The payment indicator will influence how the work is carried out and involve varying degrees of specification and supervision. For example, if payment is made by metre of trench, those people digging through rock will receive less than those digging in sand. If payment is done on time spent, people with a pattern of working slowly but over a long time may be treated differently from those who work hard and fast, but then rest for longer. The scale of payments may also have an impact; buying sand in small batches enables small-scale suppliers to provide the material; insisting on one large delivery will exclude them.

Participation in construction

Many development projects expect people to contribute either in terms of labour and local materials or financially. Nobody likes to work for free but those with a lower status in society will have less opportunity to avoid 'volunteering'. Thus women are often expected to do voluntary work or get involved in peripheral activities such as preparing food for the project team. However, there is plenty of scope at this stage of the project cycle for giving women real chances to be fully involved and thus feel empowered and valued. Participation in the construction of a project also leads naturally into the maintenance of the works. If somebody has

Inclusion by design

"In one area, men traditionally built walls whilst women plastered them. In an effort to get women involved in the construction of buildings, techniques that were based on plastering, such as ferro-cement, were used so women could be involved without unnecessarily disrupting local practices."

Rebecca Scott, WEDC

"A social scientist originally wanted the construction of a water system in a peri-urban area to be carried out by voluntary labour, to 'give ownership of the project' to the community. The engineer was not happy as this would mean more supervision, technical training (for people who would only need the skills once), erratic work rates and potential problems with quality.

Further investigation of the community revealed that the poor in the peri-urban population worked in a cash economy and could not afford to give up work to provide labour. Working after work would lengthen an already long day. By having a cash contribution instead, the social scientist's request for 'ownership' was fulfilled and the engineer could employ builders to carry out the work. The builders employed local people to carry out labouring jobs on the site. A significant proportion of the labourers were poor women. Although they still ended up working on the project, they were now being paid rather than being pressured to provide their time for free."

Brian Reed, WEDC

been involved in the construction of infrastructure, they will have more experience, knowledge and confidence when it needs repairing, altering or re-building.

Using community labour may reduce labour costs, but the increased time and supervision required may outweigh direct cost savings. Involving the community should therefore also contribute to other project goals, such as ownership or maintenance.

Division of labour

In both formal and voluntary construction, women will often tend to be allocated to the unskilled but heavy work such as transporting or breaking stones, carrying sand or digging, or marginal work such as cooking for the labourers. Men will take the skilled (and often better paid) jobs and this may make women feel excluded or under-valued in the project.

Both engineers and inexperienced local people may have preconceptions about what they can and cannot do on a construction site. If inclusive employment policies are being used, the engineer may not only have to provide some training for women, but also make positive efforts to show that they can do the work. Examples from similar projects are good illustrations for what people unused to building can achieve. Part-time work may be more inclusive than only offering full-time jobs.

"A large water supply project had a requirement to involve women in the scheme. The majority of the construction stage had to be tendered for internationally according to the policy of the funding agency.

The companies likely to tender would be managed by men and employ men for the majority of the responsible tasks. Women's involvement was therefore going to be limited to commenting on the plans and then operating the system after construction.

A small proportion of the funds could be spent locally however. Construction contracts to protect springs were let to local self-employed artisans. These men (they were all men) employed people locally to help with the labouring and to supply materials such as building stone and sand. Significant proportions of these labourers were local women, who managed to fit the work around their other tasks. Some of the funds being paid to the artisans were therefore being transferred to women in the local community, especially the poor. This would not be the case with a large contractor, who would contract full-time staff and buy materials in bulk.

The use of local artisans also enabled the local community to comment on and monitor the construction process, as they knew the people working on each spring. Slow work rates at one site were reported to the project staff by the women who still used the spring for water supply.

One businesswoman took more active steps to get involved. She bid for a contract to build a spring and employed an artisan to carry out the work."

Brian Reed, WEDC

In any community, certain tasks will be specific to men or women; engineers will not necessarily be aware of this, but should try to understand what the differences are. Many tasks can be carried out by men or women, but perhaps in different ways. For instance, both men and women can carry similar amounts of material; women may carry many small loads on their heads, or work in pairs, whilst men may carry larger loads, possibly in wheelbarrows, but alone and take longer rests. This can be used to advantage if women are employed transporting small separate loads, and men take care of the larger quantities. For example women may be primary collectors of waste, take this to a collection point and men then transport this to the disposal site.

There are some practical points that construction managers can do to make construction open to all the community:

- job descriptions should be written carefully to avoid bias towards men or women;
- pay structures should be clear and transparent so that all employees know they are getting paid the same for comparable work;
- women may benefit from being paid by piecework because this gives them the flexibility to work and attend to domestic chores;
- piecework has to be equal. If men dig trenches in rocky ground and women dig in lighter soils, the men need to have the extra effort recognised;
- care should be taken about allocating work on a household basis, as this may cause problems for female-headed households;
- contracts can be broken into small packages. Local contractors are likely to be small and less able to tender for large contracts;

"In 1991, the Project Urban Self Help (PUSH) involved the World Food Programme with the Government of Zambia giving 'food for work' in the shantytown infrastructure-upgrading project in the townships of Lusaka. As there was a large workforce previously unskilled in construction and only a limited number of engineers and technicians, there was an obvious need for training of staff and members of the workforce.

The majority of the workforce was female and most of these women had been denied schooling from an early age. Many of the men had also had limited education as the majority of the workers were from the poorer sector of the community. A range of training courses were arranged in the local languages and in English.

Courses started at the most basic level and progressed to technician and engineer level. The training courses were extremely well received especially by the women.

One female worker said

"I had wanted to be a nurse but I had to leave school to be married and now I have many children and it is not possible"

The training courses were received enthusiastically with reference to what was learnt, but they also offered an opportunity for the women to support each other in their learning and in confidence building. They also ended in shows of much excitement as certificates were handed out. One of the most important factors in any training course was that the trainee's abilities were built upon and never criticised. Emphasis was placed on positive comments and discussions of improvements to methods etc. With this atmosphere, the trainees soon began to speak out, as they were not frightened of being put down or criticised. Training courses were mainly practical based so as not to limit those with less formal education. Where written notes were provided pictures were heavily used. Notes were provided in both English and the local language for those who did not speak English. Some doubts exist over the usefulness of the printed notes; especially those in the local language; as although the intention was good, the local language is not generally written and most of those who did not speak English had not attended school and hence could not read either language. However, notes were important for those who could read and were provided for all, so there was a feeling of equal treatment."

Sarah House

94

- poor people have better social contacts with local builders than with large companies coming from outside the area;
- women do have childcare responsibilities. Providing a crèche or enabling job-sharing may allow women to work on a project;
- women may use different tools from men — lighter spades, ladders with closer rungs, small carrying pans rather than wheelbarrows, smaller work boots;
- construction managers should discuss with their employees to find out how they would carry out a task;
- women may prefer to work in groups — for social, security or cultural reasons; and
- separate toilets need to be provided for men and women.

Supervision

For cultural and social reasons it may be preferable for female workers to be supervised by women and for male workers to be supervised by men. If men and women are working on separate tasks this may happen naturally. Men and women who were involved in the previous stages of the project should also be informed of the construction progress. This will again reinforce the ownership of the project, show how the work is carried out, demonstrate the costs and give some idea of the maintenance requirements in the future.

Local people can also supervise outside contractors, as they have a vested interest in the final product.

Health and safety

Men and women may need to have different considerations for health and safety. Physical differences may mean men and women need different

Choosing your tool

Different tools and equipment can suit men and women. Spades and hammers come different sizes. Wheelbarrows can make carrying heavy objects easier.

Breaking male bastion brick by brick

A successful sanitation project needed more skilled masons to build latrines. It had been employing women to assist male masons. They trained women in construction methods. The women had been married, had children and had experience working as a mason's assistant.

The biggest problems were social, but through confidence building and working in teams, the women realised they could do this job. Some communities did not want women to come and build latrines in their area, but the quality of their work has shown people that they can produce a well-built latrine.

Thresiamma Mathew, Waterlines, Vol.17: No1, July 1988

sized protective clothes and boots. Men and women can carry different loads, so items such as cement may have to be packed in smaller bags so women can carry them without injury. In some dangerous activities, such as digging trenches, husband and wife teams work together to reinforce a safety culture and use established bonds of trust.

Operation and maintenance

Infrastructure does need to be maintained if it is going to fulfil its remit. Far too many past infrastructure projects fail to meet their development goals because of inadequate provision for their long-term sustainability. Operation and Maintenance tasks can include:

* general management;
* inspection;
* maintenance;
* refurbishment;
* replacement of parts; and
* collection of fees.

These tasks can cost between 0.25 and 10 per cent per year of the total construction costs[38], but the cost of an infrastructure failure due to poor O&M can be much greater.

The poor have a vested interest in keeping the services running. If infrastructure breaks down, the first people to experience the adverse effects will be the poor. If a pump breaks, richer people will be able to buy water from further a field. The poor will not be able to do this and the burden of collecting water from elsewhere will fall on the people who normally

---

38. *Civil Engineering procedure*, 5th ed. Institution of Civil Engineers.

Narayan's study found that the level of overall participation had little impact on the effectiveness of construction. If only participation during the construction stage was considered, the relationships were even weaker, demonstrating that participation is a long-term activity, rather than just a single event at some stage of the project. The multivariate factors that were more important to the quality of construction were economic context (0.59), project complexity (-0.30) and number of users (-0.30). So, if inflation was high, the project large and complex, the construction would suffer. One of the reasons for a low correlation with participation is the limited scope of participation at this stage. Providing unskilled, unpaid labour is not going to make best use of the community's expertise.

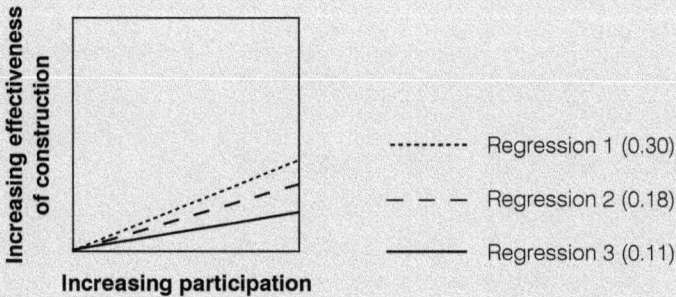

y-axis: **Increasing effectiveness of construction**

x-axis: **Increasing participation**

.... Regression 1 (0.30)

─ ─ ─ Regression 2 (0.18)

──────── Regression 3 (0.11)

A similar pattern was found with the performance of operation and maintenance. For maintenance after one year, the bivariate regression coefficient was 0.43, but the multivariate coefficients were 0.16 and 0.18, with availability of spare parts and presence of technicians being more significant. For maintenance after five years, the figures are 0.46, 0.09 and 0.25 respectively, with availability of spare parts being the only significant determinant of success.

The Contribution of People's Participation — Evidence from 121 Rural Water supply Projects, Deepa Narayan, World Bank, 1995[†]

do this — women and girls. If a road is full of potholes, the poor in buses will suffer more than the rich in 4x4 cars.

Men and women will take on different roles in operating and maintaining infrastructure services managed by the community. Traditionally the socially excluded have been involved in the mundane aspects of operation, for example the poorest in society often work on solid waste management. A common scenario for water supplies is women carrying out the daily tasks and using the system, but the responsibility for keeping the service

"In Banda Uttar Pradesh, India, women were very frustrated with the low rate, delays, and infrequency of pump repair. They organised themselves and protested at the offices of the local office of the state government's water supply organisation. Taking their water jugs, they smashed them into small clay pieces in the office compound. Finally the water department agreed to respond. In co-ordination with a women's centred NGO Mahila Samayaka, the women received technical training, and the water department agreed to help train and pay them a small stipend to repair their own pumps. After forming repair teams of three women, and providing tools and backup, the effort has been very successful, with a change from more than 50% of the pumps out of order at a time to only a nominal few out of order in the district. Mahila Samakya then followed up with other services to the women, including non-formal education. While being successful, the project has yet to find a way to collect local fees to ensure the effort will be sustained, should the water department stop paying the pump mechanic fees to the women."

Jacob Pfohl, *Mainstreaming Gender in WES,* UNICEF, 1998

Managers

Managers are required for both technical support and financial control. In Tereta, in Ethiopia, the water supply system has managers for both these tasks, but unconventionally, the technical manager is female and the financial manager is male.

running has prestige and so people in more powerful positions take on this role — without necessarily understanding the needs and priorities of the users. Positive action and training can increase the diversity of people able to take on management and maintenance tasks.

Engineers' actions

Engineers can contribute to equitable operation and maintenance in three ways:

- They can ensure the infrastructure can be maintained by men or women — it is no good employing a female caretaker if she cannot climb up to inspect raised tanks or unscrew bolts on a hand pump. These problems can be designed out by the engineer.
- Caretakers, technicians and management teams are often trained to take over the infrastructure when the construction stage of the project has finished. Engineers can ensure that women are involved in the training.
- The engineer or project manager will be involved in setting up the management structure that will manage the utility. Equity can be encouraged by obvious means, such as ensuring women make up a percentage of the management committee and are enabled to make a contribution. Engineers can also influence the management in more subtle ways, such as the design of the project.

Many of these issues will have had to be planned at the feasibility stage — it is too late to try and implement them after construction has finished. Planning for the supply of spares is an example; are spares available? is there a viable supply network? can the need for spares be reduced to reduce reliance on parts or should parts be designed so they need to be replaced frequently but at a low-cost?

Management

The on-going management of a service by the community is an obvious case of local involvement[39]. This should be planned, rather than expecting people to start devoting time to managing a system they may not have wanted or that does not suit their needs. Using existing organizations may be more efficient than setting up new institutions provided they are representative of all users (men, women and socially disadvantaged groups), that they can cope with the work and that they are motivated. Management will need help and inputs from outside the community, in

---

39. See Shouten and Moriarty, *Community Water, Community Management*, ITDG, 2003.

"Two options were prepared for a small town water supply. The low recharge rates and transmissivity of the aquifer meant that about 20 boreholes would be required to meet demand. Two options were drawn up.

- Have a well field away from the town. Pump to a central raised service reservoir to supply the whole town.

- Have a dozen small tanks around the edge of the town, each supplied by one or two boreholes.

The first option would require centralised management. The second option could be managed either centrally or by local groups – or a hybrid between the two management options. The poor, especially women, would have better access to a local management group than a centralised body."

Brian Reed, WEDC

terms of occasional technical advice, water quality monitoring or spare parts, as well as monitoring and support of the community management system, to ensure it continues to function satisfactorily. This is usually a government responsibility.

Ensuring that the management structure reflects the needs of the users responds to some of the issues encountered earlier with participation. Having a fixed number of women on a committee may only result in a token presence or give a voice to already articulate or well-connected women; this however is a improvement on no female representation at all. Having smaller groups increases the opportunities for involvement by socially excluded people, but may over-burden people with tasks that are more suitable to be carried out by a larger institution. The people themselves are best placed to choose the management structure, once they understand the tasks involved and the management options available.

Finance
The community will normally be expected to bear the cost of operation and maintenance of the infrastructure. This is critical for long-term sustainability. Staff or the management committee need to be adequately informed and trained so that they know how much money to collect, how to keep the process transparent, how to keep the books, and how to deal with routine problems. Issues include:

- What is the most suitable method of payment for users (for example rural households may have an irregular cash flow and may prefer to pay for maintenance costs in kind at harvest time, whereas poor labourers may prefer small daily or weekly payments)?
- Will men and women who use the water for business have to pay a higher charge?
- Are both men and women in the community being made aware of the activities of the committee or utility so that the process is completely transparent?
- Will there be any cross subsidy by the community to ensure everybody has access to the infrastructure? Everyone may suffer if poor people do not have access to sanitation or solid waste disposal.

There is considerable evidence that women make excellent bookkeepers and they are often trusted more with public money, as long as they are provided with the literacy and numeracy skills needed and all members of the community accept them in their role.

The same considerations apply to urban systems. It is important to consider convenient ways for the user to pay for the service – frequency, place of payment etc. This may have implications for the engineering design, e.g. pre-paid meters.

Project evaluation

In the standard project cycle, the work is carried out and then reviewed ('project evaluation') to ensure that the project objectives have been addressed. Factors such as involving men and women can be measured and lessons learnt. This in turn can feed into policy review and development. Leaving the evaluation until the end of a project however will miss the opportunity for ensuring that the current project meets its targets. It also occurs after the involvement of the engineering staff, so missing the opportunity for direct feedback to the technical team enabling them to learn lessons on improving their work.

Various levels of review are carried out; monitoring can be the routine collection and analysis of information, whilst evaluation has an aspect of judging the success of the project. Engineers and social scientists may consider evaluations differently, with engineers taking a slightly dispassionate approach to the process compared with the social scientists feeling it may be more critical — an external pronouncement of success or failure. The term *assessment* is felt to be less judgmental than *evaluation*.

Women may be under a lot of pressure from their various responsibilities, but may still take on new maintenance duties. Project staff should not make assumptions about whether women can or cannot do this, but try to assist the individuals concerned to make an informed choice.

In Lesotho one third of the households are headed by women, largely due to labour migration, with about half the men employed outside the country. As a result, women do most of the work in the house and the community including installing new water systems, digging trenches, laying pipes and carrying rocks needed to construct water reservoirs. When the government started a programme to train water minders or handpump caretakers to ensure proper use of systems, it encouraged village water committees to select women to be trained together with men. Between 1981 and 1983, of the 348 water minders trained, 115 were women.

One, a mother of six, was given a five-day training course on the importance of potable water supply, the operation of the handpump and the potential breakdowns of the hand pumps. She was also instructed in public relations, personal hygiene and environmental sanitation.

Supplied with a kit of basic tools, she returned to her village Matlohelva to take care of the system. She was also responsible for persuading her neighbours to help cut the grass around the water source and cleaning the distribution tank and seal boxes. She had to collect money from each member of the community every month to defray the cost of diesel for the engine, maintenance of spare parts, transportation and the engine attendant's wages. During the winter when the snow in the mountains lies 2 to 3 metres deep, she was to ensure that the pipes were covered with earth lest they freeze and burst.

IT Water Supply Source Book, 1996

Monitoring [40]

A system of regular monitoring through the design, construction and operation stages will help the project maintain its direction, for instance keeping gender issues on the agenda throughout the project, rather than just at the policy stage. However, the direction may not necessarily be that envisaged at the beginning of the process. Meeting demands and addressing

---

40. "[Monitoring] refers to the collecting, organising and using information about the actual situation and comparing it to the planned or expected situation." *Action Monitoring for Effectiveness*, *Technical Paper 35*, IRC, 2000.

the local context may mean the assumptions used at the beginning of the project are no longer valid. This continual re-appraisal of the project to suit the changing state of knowledge is called 'value engineering'.

Indicators

In order to assess impact and effectiveness, the evaluators will use indicators to measure outcomes. These have to be measured from the start of the project, in a baseline survey, in order to measure change. If external evaluators are engaged at the end of the project to provide an independent view of the work they will need a record of these indicators. The indicators can drive the project, so if the number of pit latrines built is a key indicator, the project may build latrines, at the expense of hygiene education or user demand.

In order to overcome some of these shortcomings, basing the indicators on the wishes of the users will ensure that the project is driven by local rather than external priorities. This debate needs to engage the whole community, as different parts of society may have different demands. Extra effort has to be made to find out the wishes of women or other socially excluded groups, as these have less access to the normal decision-making channels. Indicators should be simple to measure but not simplistic. For example, the number of women on a committee is easy to measure, but how representative they are of all women in the area and how much of a voice they have on that committee may not be so clear.

The community can be involved in assessing progress against the indicators, building up a culture of inspection, which is useful during the operation stage. The indicators should include both technical and socio-economic factors. Examples include:

- proportions of men/women (or other indicator — caste, age, religion, ethnicity as appropriate) trained as part of the project;
- proportions of men/women in paid/voluntary employment on the scheme;
- proportions of men/women in responsible decision making positions;
- time taken to carry out repairs;
- finances; and
- quantities of water/traffic/waste.

All of these indicators have gender implications, either directly or indirectly. User consultation will allow the project to prioritise the project objectives.

The donors and policy makers are also stakeholders, so their needs and objectives should be measured alongside those of the user group.

Assessment

Assessments may simply review the progress of a project or piece of work, or assess its impact and the extent to which its objectives have been achieved[41]. For these purposes, routine monitoring is supplemented by asking larger questions that may need additional data. In terms of gender issues, assessments should seek to identify any negative or positive impacts that the project has had on men or women in the community, for example[42]:

- Does this project correspond to gender priorities as set out in national, international or organisation policy documents?
- Were project objectives and indicators related to gender achieved? What were the factors most responsible for success?
- Were systematic efforts made to ensure that the project involved men and women? What steps were taken and how well did they work?
- Have roles/responsibilities changed as a result of this project? How did the project contribute to these changes?
- Has men and women's access to or control of resources changed as a result of this project?

The final assessment should be timed to reflect the long-term impact as accurately as possible. Time should be allowed for the project to be operated with reduced external support if lessons about the sustainability of the infrastructure and any changes in social status are to be learnt.

Project extensions

One purpose of an assessment exercise is to allow project extensions, to address some of the shortcomings or use opportunities to increase impact and sustainability. It may also lead to unrelated activities. Working with women on a water project gives them confidence and skills that can be transferred to educational, economic, social or health issues. This may require the project team to identify suitable opportunities and partners to work with the community on a longer-term basis.

---

41. Adapted from Gosling and Edwards, *Toolkits*, Save the Children, 1995.
42. Adapted from *Gender Issues Source Book* – UNDP World Bank, 1995.

In Bangladesh two separate handpump programmes were evaluated gender-specifically. The reported frequency of breakdowns was significantly lower for the pumps maintained by the women. The reported duration of breakdown was also lower but not significantly. Eleven percent more women than men cleaned the platform regularly. Of those who did this every day, twice as many were women. The views of the male caretakers coincided with the findings of the study. Almost three-quarters thought that women would be as effective as men at pump maintenance (Micro, 1984) These findings, while interesting, should be viewed with caution because they are based on recall of experience over a period of two years and not on monitoring. Also more than 80 percent of handpumps were located either on the land or in the house of the caretakers. A possible distorting factor is also the age of the pumps, which was not taken into account in the analysis.

Gender in Water Resources Technical Series 33E, IRC, 1998

Reporting

The output of several of these project stages will be a report. This should show how the scheme meets the promoter's objectives. These reports provide an opportunity for feedback and commenting on the assumptions and aims of previous stages. The basic data (disaggregated where appropriate to provide separate information on the project's impact on men and women, rich and poor), assumptions and investigations should be included, to support the recommendations and assist in later stages. This includes design, health and safety, environment and socio-economic criteria. Alternatives should be compared using parameters such as costs, risks and the achievement of the various programme aims, technical and social. Inputs to be made by the men and women who will use the outputs of the project should be highlighted, especially where their concerns may conflict with the programme policy or a generally accepted technical solution. The report should be written clearly without unnecessary technical, financial or socio-economic jargon, as a wide range of people may have to assess the report. Where reports are to be made to the community, it is particularly important to consider appropriate forms of communication, for example public meetings.

6

Practical solutions

In this chapter, examples of practical solutions, are given under the following headings:

- water resources and
- water supply systems etc.

Probably because of its significance in family life, the water supply and sanitation sector has been a leader in developing gender-sensitive approaches to project planning and implementation. Experiences over the last two decades have led to a broad international consensus on practical ways of involving all sections of society in the water supply and sanitation development process, but the approaches can be readily applied in other infrastructure projects.

Engineers are directly responsible for producing practical solutions, and social issues such as participation arise in that context. In Chapter 6, many of the solutions described are based on the design and building of water and sanitation services, because of their importance in domestic life, such as:

- Local people generally have useful knowledge of water rights and available water resources, including seasonal fluctuations and any practical or cultural reasons for avoiding certain sites.

- Women often choose simpler technologies that put them in control, in preference to high-tech installations that depend on outsiders when something goes wrong.

- Water supply design should consider the route people use to collect water. Women may consider delivery of water close to their home more important than other technical details. Design details such as taps can make collecting water easier.

.....continued overleaf

- Men and women may have different reasons for wanting a latrine built. Different designs can enhance the desirability of a latrine and improve the chances of it being used regularly. Cleaning latrines is often a domestic (woman's) task. Engineers can make latrines easy to clean.

- Children have particular sanitation needs, especially girls at school.

- Most solid waste is domestic in origin, so women have an important role to play in its management.

- Both men and women need to understand hygiene issues.

- Male and female farmers may have different priorities and use different technologies.

- Transport design can easily overlook the needs of the poor.

- In refugee camps security is an important issue for women.

"Poor and marginalized people usually view processes primarily as a means to secure something that can improve their circumstances. A project that does not yield a product is too expensive for them to pursue. A productless process is a very western, upper middle class, intellectual and psychological amenity good. Equally, however process matters. Processes that treat people as ends, not merely means, are empowering and more likely to produce recipient-friendly products. Process and product interact."

Reginald Herbold Green[43]

Engineers take the lead in supplying the infrastructure product and managing the process that leads to it. This chapter introduces some of the practical issues that can be considered if a more gender aware approach is taken. Water issues dominate, as they have a large impact on domestic chores, but sanitation, solid waste and transport all have gender implications.

Water resources

Water resources are a fundamental requirement for water supply and irrigation schemes. They have to be investigated very early in the project cycle and take a long time to measure and assess. A minimum of a year is

---

43. *Myth of Community*, Guijt and Shah, 1998.

needed to monitor seasonal variations, but many areas of the world have significant variations in rainfall over time. It rains on everybody, but the water flows concentrate it in specific places and men's and women's access to these water sources has an influence on vulnerability and poverty. The selection of one water source over another may limit options later in the project cycle.

Integrated water resource management aims to balance competing interests, say between agriculture and industry or environmental impact and flood control. Domestic water supply often only requires a small proportion of the water but its importance to the health and well-being of society means that it should be generally accepted to be a priority when allocating available water.

A gender-sensitive approach to water resource management will involve planners taking less of a macro approach and considering local and domestic needs. In doing this they also comply with the second Dublin Principle that 'Water development and management should be based on a participatory approach [implying that] decisions are taken at the lowest appropriate level.' Water resource investigations have to balance supply with demand. Demand is not just limited to quantity but also quality and use of the water.

Allocating supplies

A new water development has to take account of existing users and water rights and consider the complex issues involved in changing water allocations. In many countries, agriculture is the largest consumer of water. As different uses have different user groups, water resource allocation may have an impact on those groups — rich farmers using tube wells for irrigating thirsty crops may lower the water table at the expense of poor men and women using hand-dug wells. Water allocation may not be as definitive as the planner decrees; irrigation canals can be used as a source of water for domestic use and domestic use of water may include watering vegetable gardens and household livestock.

Where water is in limited supply, demand has to be managed. The limits may be due to absolute resource constraints or supply limitations such as storage, treatment or distribution capacity. Demand management should aim to distribute water equitably so everybody has an adequate supply. Demand management plans should take into account the wealth and gender differences of different social groups so that they are not disadvantaged.

In the Uttar Pradesh hills, an expert hydro-geologist with 30 years experience found that local people were more reliable in identifying underground springs than trained technicians. He thus built upon these skills introducing environment-friendly technologies in which hand pumps drew water from collection chambers fed by such springs in hilly, water scarce areas.

Uttar Pradesh UNICEF, *Mainstreaming Gender*

Water resource planning also has environmental impacts. Watershed protection may limit the use of woodland for firewood, forcing women to look elsewhere for fuel. Building dams may change river patterns, altering fishing, flooding (with its fertile silt) and navigation, with impacts on the men and women using the river as a natural resource. Draining swamps can destroy the habitats of fish, birds and plants that people use locally, and increase flooding downstream.

Local knowledge past and present

Local people will have knowledge of the availability of water in their area and be able to give anecdotal evidence of past variations. This is a very cost-effective way of gathering data. As men and women may use different water sources (for livestock watering, washing of clothes or water supply), both sexes need to be consulted if all sources are to be identified and current uses understood.

Meteorology and gender

The long lead-time required to monitor local water sources is an ideal opportunity to involve people locally in a project at an early stage. Training and employing people to monitor water resources and rainfall enables local people to engage in the work and feel that they are part of the project. Good daily records are not difficult to collect and it is cost effective to use local people for this work. Women are more suitable for this task if they are based at home with more fixed routines, whilst men may have to travel as part of their work. School children are even better, as collecting data can be built into the school routine and learning process – although provision does have to be made for school holidays. As men and women may use different water sources in different ways, it is sensible to employ women to monitor their water sources and men to monitor theirs.

Water sources

The choice of water source may be restricted by the available resources, but often people prefer one source to another for a variety of reasons.

One source or many?

Whilst a single point source may be easier to develop and manage for a project, this may not be the case for all of society. Assuming there are no geological restrictions on the location of any boreholes, people may have different requirements on the location of a groundwater source; should it be near to livestock, near homes for domestic use or irrigating gardens, or near clothes-washing and drying areas? If compromises cannot be reached, should several sources be developed? A series of low yielding hand-pumped boreholes or springs can be nearer to more people. They may take longer to pump water than a single motorised borehole, but are nearer to more people, so reducing time and effort of carrying water? Will a motorised borehole used for 'economic' activities lower the water table and cause shallower wells to dry up?

The management of several sources may be diffuse, but the poor are more likely to have a voice at a neighbourhood level than trying to get their views listened to at a municipal level. However, can the community

---

What do people want?

In preparing a project supported by several UN agencies in North Tanzania, the following technique was used for a quick and gender-specific assessment:

"The identification team consisting of women and men sub-divided the proposed project area into zones that differed in ecological, socio-economic and cultural conditions. It selected a small number of villages in each zone. It paid one visit to each village, met the authorities and representatives from local women's and men's organisations, explained the purpose and asked for a separate men's and women's meeting. For the meetings the team split up: the men sat with the men, the women with the women. A checklist developed by all team members helped to structure the discussion in the meetings. The discussions revealed marked gender differences in water use and needs: men used water for their cattle and needed more appropriate water points for this purpose; women needed a more reliable water supply, nearer to their homes, for domestic purposes."

Working with Women and Men, Occasional Paper 25, IRC, 1994

afford to operate and manage several sources? A variety of supplies can reduce conflicts over water and enable different activities to use different sources.

Rainwater harvesting

Rainwater harvesting does not have a high status and is often seen as a low-technology option, difficult and costly to implement as each building has to be treated as a separate site. This has made rainwater harvesting appear to be an alternative that should only be considered if other water resources are not viable. The seasonal and unpredictable nature of the resource makes formal planning difficult.

The very factors that make rainwater collection a low priority for planners make it attractive to poor householders, especially women. It is located in the household, making collection simple and safe (see Figure 6.1). It is 'free' once the capital costs are paid (benefiting women who look after the domestic budget). The technology options are varied and can be upgraded – starting with a bucket or two under the eaves and progressing to large storage tanks with water quality improvement measures. The technology is also simple and can be understood and constructed by men or women without formal building skills. Management of the system is entirely with the householder and so free from political or financial dependence on outsiders. It is however a seasonal supply and alternative sources may be required to supplement it — rather than rainwater supplementing other,

Figure 6.1. Rainwater collection takes place at home

more formal water sources. Also there are water quality problems with collecting water off thatched roofs, which tend to be the type of roof material which poor and vulnerable households can afford.

Groundwater

Groundwater is a good water resource because it is generally well protected from bacteriological pollution (unlike surface water) and has reduced seasonal variations. Some groundwater however has poor chemical water quality, including fluoride and arsenic, which can only be detected by tests and have serious long-term effects on health.

The variety of technologies allow boreholes to be upgraded over time, but they do require different levels of skill and support to maintain them, so the technical selection of options needs to be balanced with an assessment of the human resources available.

Springs

Protected springs offer a low technology, cheap source of water, but at a fixed location. Women collecting water or going to the water source to wash clothes will have to walk to the spring. Before selecting a spring for protection, consider if the location can be improved — either by piping the water somewhere more convenient or improving the route to the spring. This makes it easier to get to and women are not exposed to risks such as physical violence or carrying heavy loads up steep or slippery paths.

Surface water

Rivers and lakes are used for fishing, power generation, navigation and waste disposal as well as water abstraction for domestic, industrial and agricultural uses, each use varying with the season. This range of uses makes competition for the water more complex, as Figure 6.2 shows. Analysis of who uses water, when it is used and how it is used is essential if a picture of present water resource use is to be trusted.

Dams

The high capital cost of dams means that they are usually used for explicit economic development (irrigation and industry). The World Commission on Dams report[44] catalogues the costs and benefits of the construction of large dams. It records adverse impacts on socially excluded groups,

---

44. *Dams and Development, a new framework for decision-making,* The Report of the World Commission on Dams, 2000.

Figure 6.2. Multiple uses of water point

but says the key social indicator in many cases was tribal or racial. All members of society, rich and poor, men and women suffered due to inadequate consideration of the needs of people being affected locally by the construction of large dams. The forced migration of people hits the most vulnerable hardest as they rely on land-based livelihoods and have fewer resources, such as financial capital, education or social contacts to help them establish new livelihoods. The World Commission on Dams gives guidelines on how large dam projects should proceed. Small dams may be an appropriate community level solution to problems of varying river flow, allowing high flows to be stored for a range of possible uses when natural river flows are low or zero.

Wetlands
Wetlands and swamps are not often considered in water resource evaluations, although their use in flood control and treatment of polluted runoff is increasing. Protecting wetlands can have a big impact on poor people living in areas prone to inundation, whose livelihoods would suffer if the wetland were drained.

Research in Nkayi, Zimbabwe, showed that only men were on dam committees (for cattle watering); whereas hand-dug wells, used primarily for domestic purposes, were almost the exclusive domain of women. At boreholes, used for both purposes, the user profile was mixed and conflicts arose over the priorities of different users, with cattle watering generally taking precedence over domestic use.

(Cleaver, 1991), Gatekeeper Series No SA49, IIED,1995

Recycling

Particularly in water-short areas, water recycling may need to be taken into consideration. Even on a domestic scale, water may be used several times, for washing people then clothes then floors then disposed of by watering crops. Promoting recycling may reduce the burden of collecting water. Where water is recycled within pipe systems (for example saving water from baths to flush toilets), maintenance is required, which may add to domestic chores or cause a health risk if neglected. As a domestic activity, this needs to relate to the domestic, not community, environment.

Water source selection

Water sources are selected on a variety of criteria:

- variability;
- quality;
- location;
- existing use and users; and
- quantity.

Water resource planners will want to select the most suitable source – but this suitability may be based on their assumed priorities or 'text book' examples. Communities, households and individuals may already use a complex variety of water sources to meet their needs and a single improved source may not be able to balance the community's criteria. A supply that provides year round, clean water may seem to be the 'best' source – but if it is in the wrong location or is too expensive to use, people may prefer to use intermittent, lower quality water for some uses. Bathing requires privacy, laundry somewhere sociable to meet other women and exchange information, whilst stock watering needs easy access.

"A small town was provided with a water supply, aimed at providing 20l per person per day. The scheme was not financially viable because people still used traditional sources of water in conjunction with the piped supply. So whereas a few litres were bought for drinking and cooking, washing and laundry was carried out using 'free' water from rivers and ponds."

Joy Morgan, WELL study 323A

Definitions of quality vary. Taste, appearance, temperature and flow rate may mean one water source has a perceived higher quality and is worth the further walk to collect water for drinking or cooking.

Location of source

Water rights are often tied to land rights – especially for irrigation schemes. Where land is inequitably distributed, selecting a water source to suit influential people may further exclude the poor from any benefits. Land rights are sometimes only in men's names, so female-headed households have less access to land and water.

One of the burdens on women in managing water supplies is carrying water from the water source. Ease of access (in terms of both distance and risk of attack) can be an important consideration in selecting the source, as Figure 6.3 shows.

Meeting demand

Water resource planners try to meet demand in the engineering sense of litres per person per day. Text books often give figures for water use but these volumes mask who is using the water and where it is being used.

"A small town in western Uganda relied on one main handpump. Water vendors would have to queue to collect water. A surface water pond had no queue but was further away and people would not pay such high prices for the water, as it was not so clean. Vendors balanced the time taken and the income they could make from each source."

Brian Reed, WEDC

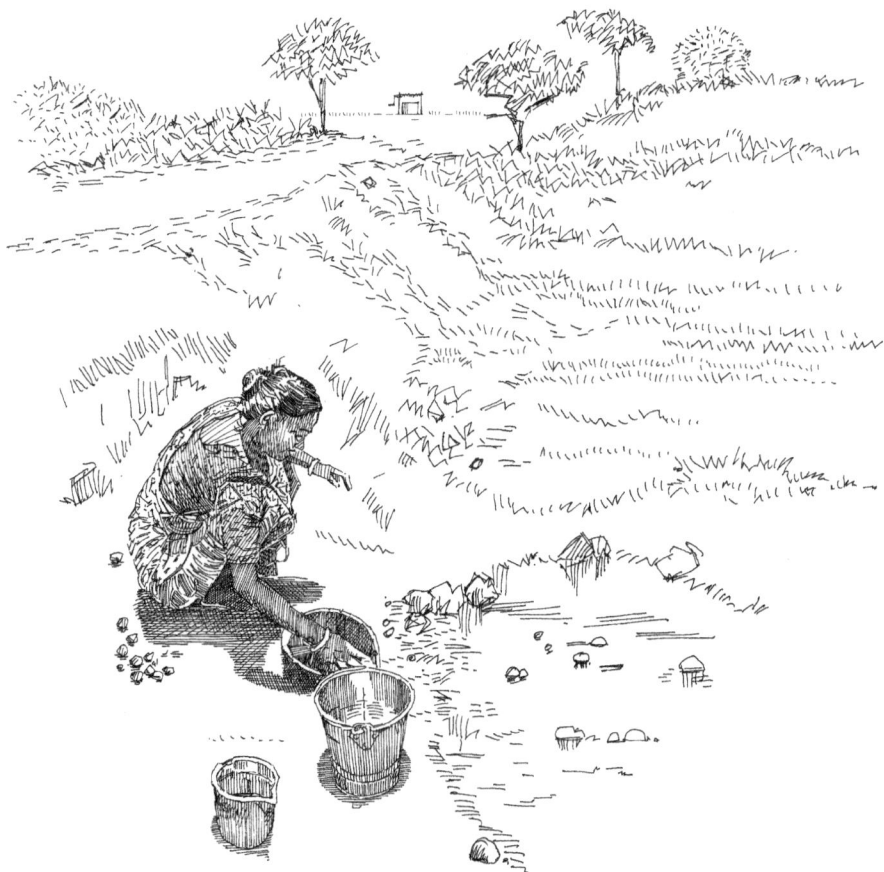

Figure 6.3. Which source would you use?

Examples of gender-related demand include:

- irrigation: men using water in formal agriculture and for livestock, women using water for subsistence and informal agriculture;
- water supply: women using water for laundry;
- sanitation: women collecting water for pour-flush latrines used by the whole family; and
- business: women using water for food preparation or brewing, men for washing vehicles.

Demand is related to both quantity and quality. Washing cars or irrigation does not need such a high quality as drinking or cooking, so men and women may demand different standards.

Quantity

Water demand in the economic sense is also dependent on the cost to the user. Apart from the financial and economic issues of ability and willingness to pay, there are the other, non-monetary costs, such as time and effort spent collecting water. Reducing all the costs can increase the quantity of water consumed. Women who take more than 30 minutes to collect water are likely to limit the amount to a 'survival supply' — say 5-15 litres per person per day (l/c/d). Neighbourhood supplies can increase this to 15-50 l/c/d, a tap outside the house to 20-80 l/c/d and a tap inside the house to 30-250 l/c/d. It is not just the distance that is important but also the time walking to and from the source, the queuing time and the time taken to fill the container, as shown in Figure 6.4[45].

The quantity of water available has an impact on hygiene. Once the water for drinking has been satisfied, people can use extra water for more regular washing of utensils, people and clothes. Bathing and washing clothes near the water source reduces the burden of carrying water home. Increased cleanliness reduces disease — of benefit to all, especially the sick and to those people who have to look after them.

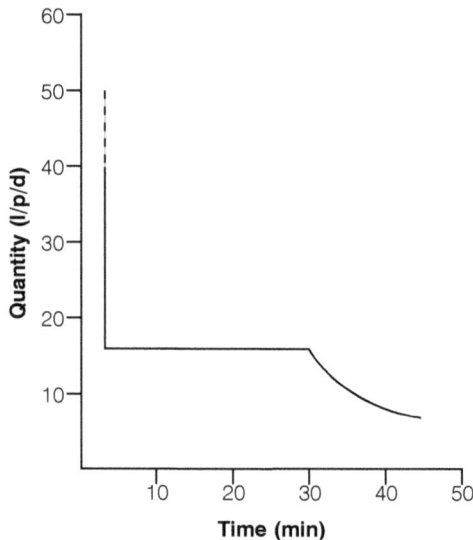

Figure 6.4. Water consumption vs time for collection

45. From Cairncross and Feachem, *Environmental Health Engineering in the Tropics,* 2nd edition, 1993.

Water supply systems[46]

Once a water source has been selected, the water supply system can be designed. For surface water sources, this normally consists of treatment and distribution systems, with storage at various stages to balance seasonal and diurnal variations in supply and demand. Women are often the users of water domestically and so are likely to be concerned with the design and operation of a water supply scheme. Women and children are the main collectors of water so they are likely to benefit from reduced physical strain, less time spent collecting water (including time queuing) and from increased family health that improved water supplies can provide. The importance of women's roles in managing existing water supplies is the stimulus for involving women in improving the water supply and, in turn, using this opportunity for longer-term strategic actions, such as literacy education or confidence building.

Wells, boreholes and handpumps

The technical options for exploiting groundwater vary, including:

- open wells;
- covered wells with a pump;
- boreholes with a handpump;
- boreholes with a motorised pump, windpump or solar pump; and
- springs with protection works.

Influencing local policy

In Guatemala's Three Crowns Community in Totonicapan the NGO 'Water for the People' encountered a serious problem with the drinking water. The men refused to take any initiative in solving the problem, as domestic water is not their priority. The women leaders of the community formed a committee, looked for better water sources, prepared legal documents needed to acquire the land and looked for funding from external sources. Once the women were able to get funds, the men began to believe in the women's work and began to support them. Now they are part of the committee. They do the construction, but the women continue their management function.

IT Water Supply Source Book, 1996

---

46. For more information see *Small-scale Water Supply – A Review of Technologies*, Skinner, B. ITDG, UK 2003.

Figure 6.5. How high should a well wall be?

There are many options that need to be discussed with the community that may influence technical decisions.

Wells are simple technically, but can be designed to suit the needs of the water collectors. Subject to geophysical limitations, they should be sited according to the demands of the water collectors. Well digging is often a task that men carry out, so excluding men from a project by focusing solely on women may limit options and the benefit of practical experience. Discussing a simple technical issue, such as the height of the well wall with women may encourage them to talk about other related issues (as shown in Figure 6.5).

Handpumps are technically more demanding than simple wells. The mechanical nature of the handpump used to mean that men were selected to be trained as technicians. However, men do not have access to the same social networks as women. These are needed to persuade people to keep the areas around the handpump clean and report pump failures. It may be better to balance the number of men and women involved in pump maintenance, so that their social strengths and weakness can complement each other.

Selecting the type and location of handpumps needs to take into consideration the physical requirements of the user — one size may not fit everybody. The rower pump in Figure 6.6 shows how different people will use the same pump but in a different way.

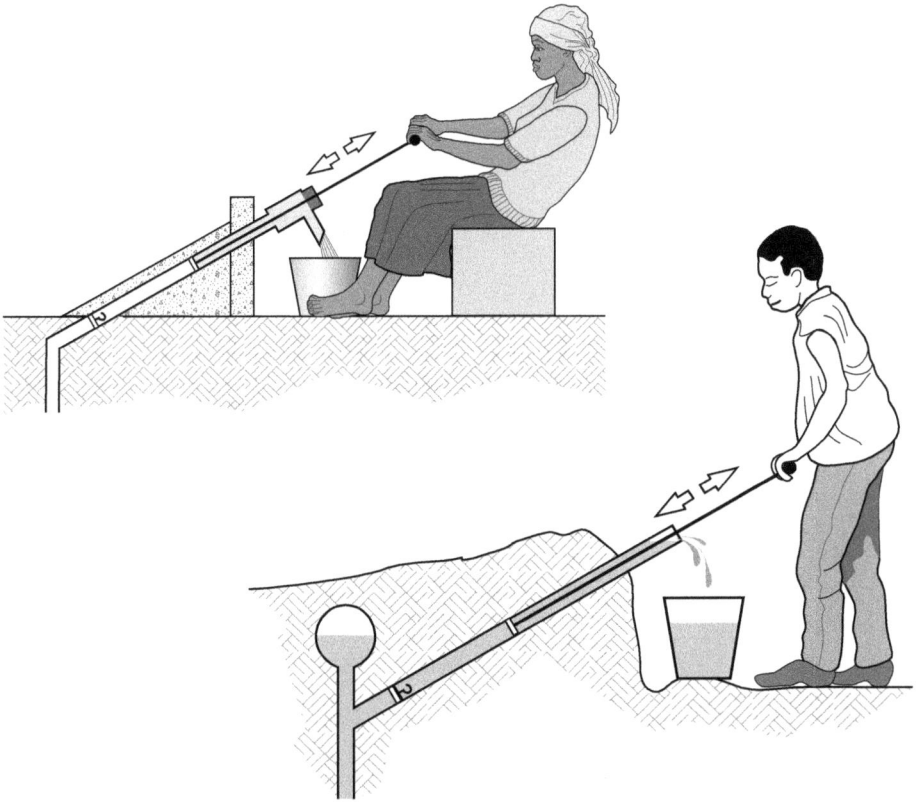

Figure 6.6. Arrangements of the rower pump to suit users' needs

Are handpumps designed for women and disabled people?

Springs

Protected springs are a local, low technology system that is easy to understand and maintain. The layout of the walls and paths can make it easier for women and children to walk to the spring (and return with heavy loads), keep the area clean and provide areas for washing and drying clothes. A handrail may make steps easier, as shown in Figure 6.7. A tank may reduce the time women and children waste in queuing for water at times of peak demand.

Figure 6.7. A protected spring

122

Treatment

Treating water is complex, costly and requires skill and knowledge. If men and women are to be involved in the project, they will need to be able to manage the water treatment. An alternative is to reduce the amount of treatment, thus removing barriers to participation. The water resources may have to be re-visited to see if better quality sources are available. It may often be easier for the community to set up groundwater protection zones or restrict access to catchments than manage complex treatment systems. Replacing one active treatment stage with a passive water quality protection measure can reduce the burden on the men and women running the system. Figure 6.8 shows how a simple groundwater protection zone is technically much simpler than a water treatment system.

Treatment can also be moved further down the supply chain. Rather than treat all water whatever it is going to be used for, or where water can be polluted once it has been treated (either in the distribution system or once it has been collected from the system), consider household level treatments, such as disinfection or iron removal. This will devolve responsibility to those best able to manage their water supply and target resources more effectively. However, it may increase financial burdens on the end user and increased workload for women as the usual custodians of water so it should be carefully discussed.

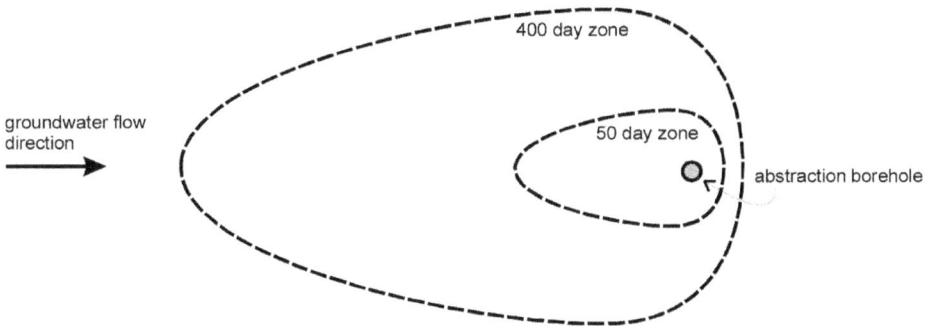

Figure 6.8. A groundwater protection zone

Distribution

Storage

Storage is required to even out seasonal and diurnal variations in supply and demand. Lack of storage can mean long queues for water at certain times (increasing the problems for those collecting it) or lack of water when it may be most useful (e.g. extending the growing season). Storage may also mean people do not have to travel as far to collect water or use less suitable sources in the dry season.

The size, location, number and material of the service reservoirs can have social and economic implications. Some issues to consider include:

- Single, centralised reservoirs tend to be managed centrally, with less opportunity for local opinions to be taken into consideration.
- Siting reservoirs to feed gravity systems should allow all people to receive water. People on the edge of the supply zone may experience problems with low pressures or infrequent supply.
- Small reservoirs can help provide an equitable supply by controlling the amount of water consumed by people served by each tank. Using locally owned tanks can reduce the size of public service reservoirs.
- Large, elevated reservoirs need higher levels of skill to design, build and repair than smaller, low-level tanks.
- Reinforced concrete or steel tanks may need more expertise to construct than locally built masonry or ferro-cement tanks. Small, off-the-shelf plastic tanks may be more expensive than a concrete equivalent, but people may find it easier to raise money than rely on external professional staff.
- Several small tanks are more robust than a single large tank. If a large tank is damaged, it is not only more expensive to replace, but the income stream is also interrupted. A collection of small tanks can continue to provide a service and income whilst a single tank is being repaired or replaced. The cost of single small tank is more manageable than a large tank, even though the sum total of all the small tanks may be greater than a single tank.
- Several small tanks can even out demand in the transmission system, reducing the pipe sizes needed. Reduced pressures also reduce leakage.
- Using elevated service reservoirs may cause problems for women if they have to climb up to maintain them. Clothes and culture may make it 'unseemly' to climb ladders to inspect the tank, record water levels or dose with chemicals.

Storage is also needed in the home. Poorer people are less likely to have many good storage vessels. This affects the quality and quantity of water stored. Lack of storage means more frequent trips to collect water and generally lower levels of water use.

Trickle feed tanks

An innovative system has been developed in South Africa to give households more control over their water supplies. Each household has a tank with an orifice that limits the flow into the tank. The household pays for a daily quota depending on the size of the orifice. This gives a low-cost mechanism for charging by volume without metering. It brings water supplies to people, increasing the quantity and quality of water available.

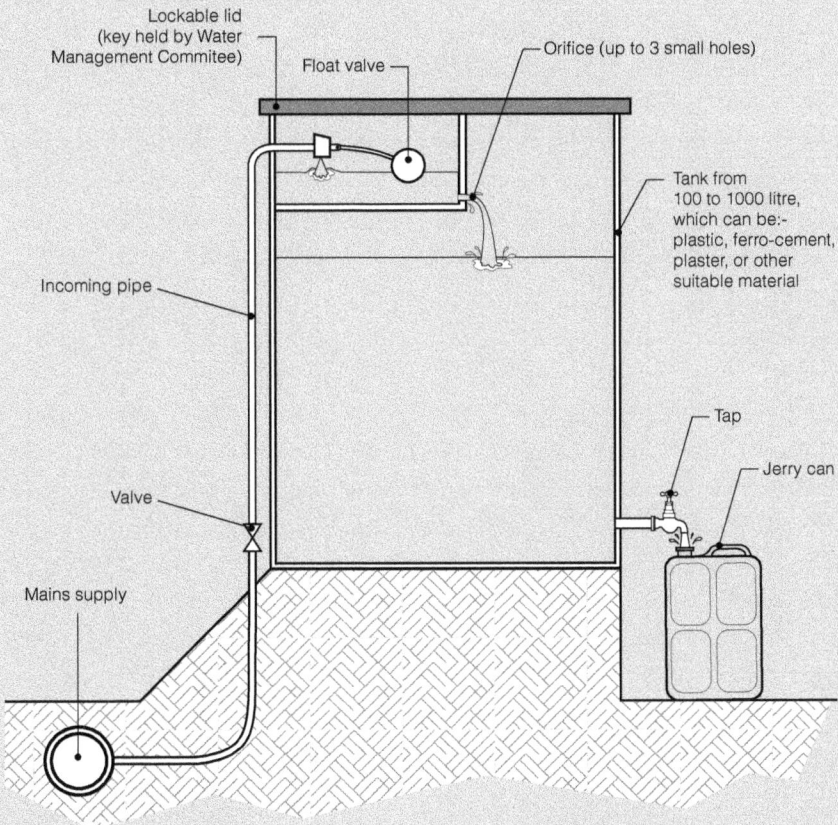

Lockable lid (key held by Water Management Commitee)

Float valve

Orifice (up to 3 small holes)

Tank from 100 to 1000 litre, which can be:- plastic, ferro-cement, plaster, or other suitable material

Incoming pipe

Tap

Jerry can

Valve

Mains supply

Jonathan Tipping and Rebecca Scott, 27th WEDC International Conference

Pipes

Piping water reduces collection problems in terms of time, distance, physical effort, exposure to risks, and contamination of the source or collected water. This reduces the burdens on those who collect the water, so women can benefit from a good distribution system. By improving both the quality and quantity of water collected, it also brings health benefits.

Designing and constructing gravity piped water systems is a relatively simple exercise, avoiding some of the educational and physical barriers that may exclude people from more complex tasks such as drilling a borehole or running treatment systems. Local knowledge of the terrain by those people who regularly collect water may assist the designers in selecting the most appropriate route.

In some cultures women have the responsibility for digging in the fields, so employing women in the construction of the trenches may not only be culturally more acceptable than using men, but the income is more likely to benefit the whole household. The activity can provide an entry point for more strategic gender issues and also offer a route for women to gain more skilled jobs on the project. Involving women in the building will also help them in any operation or repair tasks required later. Not only will women have a vested interest in keeping the system working, but also the female-based social networks can help the reporting of leaks and supply problems.

Delivery

The delivery point for water supplies can have social implications. The water point has to be accessible to all. In some cultures certain classes or castes may not be allowed to use the same area, so two or more supply points will be required. The locations of the supply points can easily be influenced by the more vocal local voices and thus favour the politically adept rather than the poor. Water collection can be an important social activity, providing an opportunity for communication among women who may have limited opportunities for meeting elsewhere.

Delivery points also depend on the water uses — specific delivery points are useful for animal watering, washing (people, clothes or vehicles) and domestic supply. This reduces conflicts, helps equitable allocation and payment and allows selective treatment. Where the delivery is at the source (e.g. river or spring) these issues need to be handled in a different manner (e.g. timed access for different uses).

The design of the tap-stand or spring spout also needs consideration. Potential pitfalls include[47]:

- spouts that are so short the water falls onto the rim of the collection vessel;
- uneven surfaces so you cannot rest the collection vessel when filling it;
- too small a distance between the spout and the ground, so water has to be transferred from a small vessel to the larger collection vessel; (Figure 6.9) and
- the height that women and children have to lift full water pots to put them onto their heads or backs.

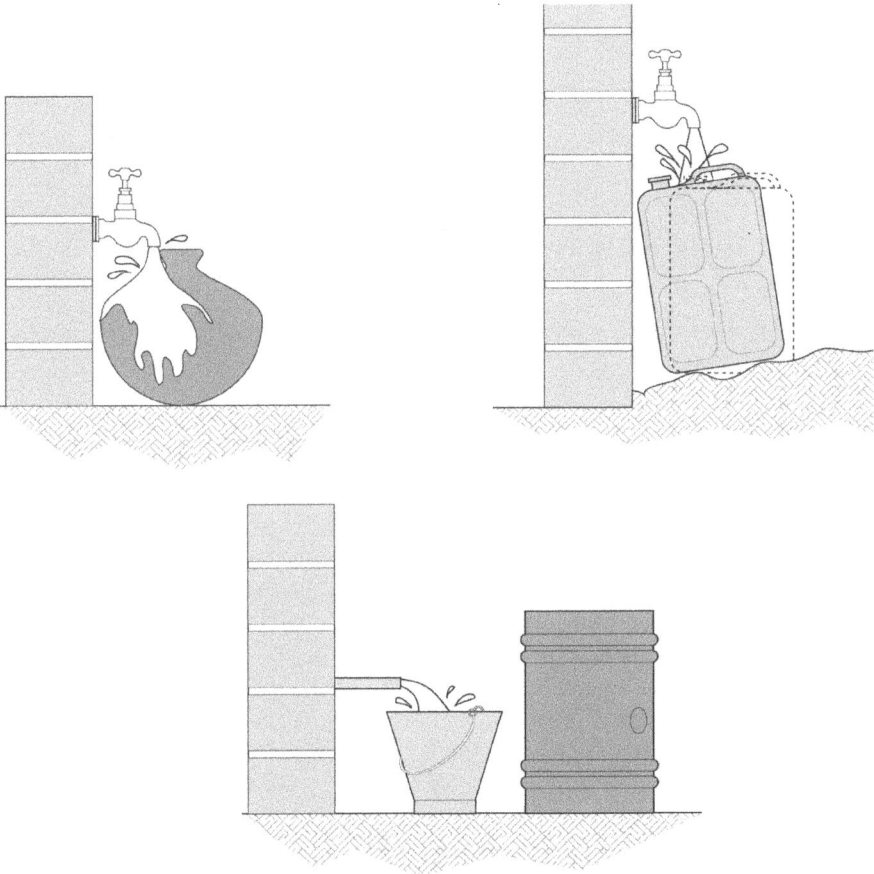

Figure 6.9. Problems with taps

47. Personal communication from Renu Gera, UNICEF India.

Figure 6.10. The tap should reflect users' needs

The location of water points matters

"In all the communities involved in the Nepal research, women complained that their water collection time significantly increased (nearly 400-500%) after they received the improved water services. This is because the tap stands and the tube wells are located along the roadside, where they cannot bathe freely and wash their clothes used during menstruation comfortably, for shame of being seen by males. In order to avoid this, women in Hile village in east Nepal, (which is in the hills and therefore cold) carry water all the way to their homes several times each day, spending significant amounts of energy to do this. In three villages on the Tarai plain (Motipur, Magaragadhi, and Gajedi), women reported waiting until dark to undertake these activities. They said they did not have this problem when they had used the more distant traditional sources, where there was no chance of men being around. All these women also complained that the surveyors had not involved them in designing the tap stands or tube wells themselves."

Shibesh Chandra Regmi and Ben Fawcett, *Gender and Development*, Vol 7.3, November 1999, pp62-72. Oxfam, Oxford

Although the usual image of water collectors is of women and children, men can be involved. Where people pay for water delivered to their house, the water vendors are often young men. Excluding their needs in the design of water points may hamper their livelihoods and cause problems for those who depend on vendors for their water supply. Vendors generally use larger containers and bicycles or carts for transporting water.

Figure 6.11. A variety of carrying containers

Carrying water

The engineer's responsibility often ends at the tap. The burden on women and children who have to carry the water starts at this point. The choice of container affects the load on the people carrying the water – a full 20-litre jerry can weighs more than 20kg. The type of container can also have an effect on the quality of the water. Large open jars where people put their hands on the lip of the container are more readily contaminated than closed containers that can be sealed. If the water is stored in the home in the same container as it is carried in, then there is less opportunity for contamination. Changing people's choice of container may improve the burden and quality of the water, but is dependent on the preference of the user.

Payment

The economic value of water has been recognised in the Dublin Principles and cost recovery is an important part of the financial sustainability of water systems. Men and women, rich and poor have different access to financial assets. Poor people's cash income is often seasonal or erratic, with no access to credit or large sums. Men generally have responsibility for 'capital' payments (e.g. a household water connection) while women are responsible for household expenditure (e.g. paying water bills), even though they may have no control over household finance. Enabling poor people to pay for house connections over several months through an increased tariff may increase access to water but shift the payment burden from men to women.

Some payment systems allow large accounts to be settled monthly in arrears, with discounts for bulk supplies, whilst small accounts have to be paid daily with no discount. This can mean that the poor, without the benefit of credit, pay more per cubic metre of water than rich people.

Environmental sanitation[48]

Environmental sanitation is the management of all factors in the environment that can cause problems to human health, so this includes engineering issues such as drainage and solid waste management, as well as the more specific area of *sanitation*, which is the safe management of human excreta. We have to consider both the hardware (e.g. latrines and sewers)

---

48. For more information see *A guide to the Development of On-Site Sanitation*. Franceys, R., Pickford, J. & Reed, R. WHO, 1992.

and software (e.g. promotion, regulation and hygiene education). The design of sanitation has to take into account both social gender differences (such as control of household finances or responsibility for cleaning) and the sexual differences (women menstruate, men can use urinals).

Environmental sanitation involves both public and private infrastructure. Householders provide the private element of the service, as they install the latrine, toilet, sink or solid waste receptacle. This is a clear case of having to involve the householder in planning and managing the system. Often roles are divided within a household, with men responsible for capital works and women managing the maintenance, so involvement of both parties is essential. To increase sanitation coverage, the project may have to promote better sanitation — hardware and software — to persuade householders to provide their part of the system. The hardware can be either on-plot[49] or sewered[50] systems. The software often includes hygiene promotion.

Promotion of sanitation

As in any marketing exercise, the project manager has to find out what will encourage people to change their current practices. Although planners may want to promote sanitation to improve the health of a population, the motivating factors for men, women and children may be different. Although health benefits are important socially and economically, they are rarely the priority of the community.

Meeting the demands of men

Where men control major household expenditure it will be important to convince them of the need to provide or improve household sanitation. Status might be an important factor in why men may choose to install a toilet. For example there may be a desire to be seen to be 'modern' or to be 'rich' or avoid the embarrassment of not being able to offer the use of a good latrine to visitors. In some communities, a latrine is increasingly being considered by brides and in-laws as an important feature at the home of a prospective husband. Where status is an important desire, prospective owners may reject some low-cost sanitation options.

---

49. On plot: sanitation where the excreta are collected, treated and disposed of within the household boundary. Includes pit latrines and septic tanks.
50. Sewers: excreta are flushed along sewer pipes using water, to be collected, treated and disposed of off site.

"Probably the most common reason given for not having a latrine is that householders cannot afford them, or claim they cannot. As they usually have to pay, rural men have to be convinced of the value of sanitation. Their only experience of latrines may be the dirty public ones at railway stations and lorry parks, so they do not think latrines encourage cleanliness. Fit and hard-working farmers see no evidence that sanitation improves health if they compare themselves with latrine-using townspeople. The only valid reason for latrines they see may be that latrines may provide fertilizer.

'Gender issues' are often mentioned in relation to sanitation, emphasising the importance of the 'role of women'. So it is interesting to read that most men in a sanitation programme in the Philippines admitted that they had been convinced to join by their wives or mothers. Men in northern Pakistan said that the reason for installing latrines was to provide privacy for women rather than for health or hygiene considerations"[51]

Meeting the demands of women

Often the most important issues for women are those of privacy and convenience. In some cultures, the need for privacy means women without access to sanitation suppress urination and defecation until after nightfall to the detriment of their health. Personal safety is also important, as going out at night to urinate or defecate in the open or at a communal toilet can expose women to rape or violence. This is a particularly strong concern of women, but men's fear for the safety of their wives and daughters can also be a powerful incentive to build a domestic latrine. The convenience of having a latrine close at hand during illness and rainy weather is a good selling point. This is also important for elderly people and those with a disability.

Menstruation is an issue that clearly affects women and should be catered for when sanitation facilities are provided.

Meeting the demands of children

Children can feel unsafe when entering darkened rooms or squatting or sitting over pits. Locating the latrine somewhere 'safe' and convenient, with a slab or pedestal that relates to children's sizes and providing doors that they can use easily are all issues that can encourage children to use the latrine. Covers for squat holes and lids for pedestals may stop children

---

51. *Low cost sanitation*, Chapter 3, John Pickford, WEDC.

falling into the pit. Disposal of babies' excreta is important for preventing disease. Potties need to be emptied into a latrine. Washable nappies will contaminate laundry wastewater and disposable nappies will add faecal matter to solid waste.

Local Kenyan cultural practices

"In the Giriama community of Kenya, it is taboo for the parents-in-law to use the same sanitation facilities as their son's wife. This was not fully appreciated at first, and lead to under utilisation of facilities."

Wamira Appollo, WEDC student, 1996

Factors underlying latrine demand in Kerala

Men's comments on constructing latrines:

- A latrine was a felt need for me, but I thought I could not afford one.
- I was unaware of the possibilities of low cost latrines.
- Local masons and others always mentioned septic tank latrines that are not affordable. I had always wanted a latrine for my family but suitable technology was not known or available.
- Until recently there was enough land near my house, now new houses have come up and going to the open air is difficult.
- By using latrines we can control disease and save money on medical consultations. Having a good latrine increases the value of the property.

Women's comments on constructing latrines:

- Men can go out at any time, we have to wait for darkness for passing urine and defecation and have to control our diet for this. We have to go to the beach or canal sides for outside area defecation, but when one is seriously ill this becomes a problem.
- Many a time diarrhoea and dysentery have affected our family.
- My grown up daughter going to college started demanding one
- The water committee members continue to insist on cleanliness and use of latrines. The fly control campaign also mentioned latrines.
- We went to our future daughter-in-laws and saw a good latrine there. Indirectly they asked about our facilities. Our friends have good latrines.
- As women we are prone to be teased when we go outside for defecation.

Kurup et al., 1996 in *Gender in Water Resources,* Technical Paper Series 33ED, IRC,1998

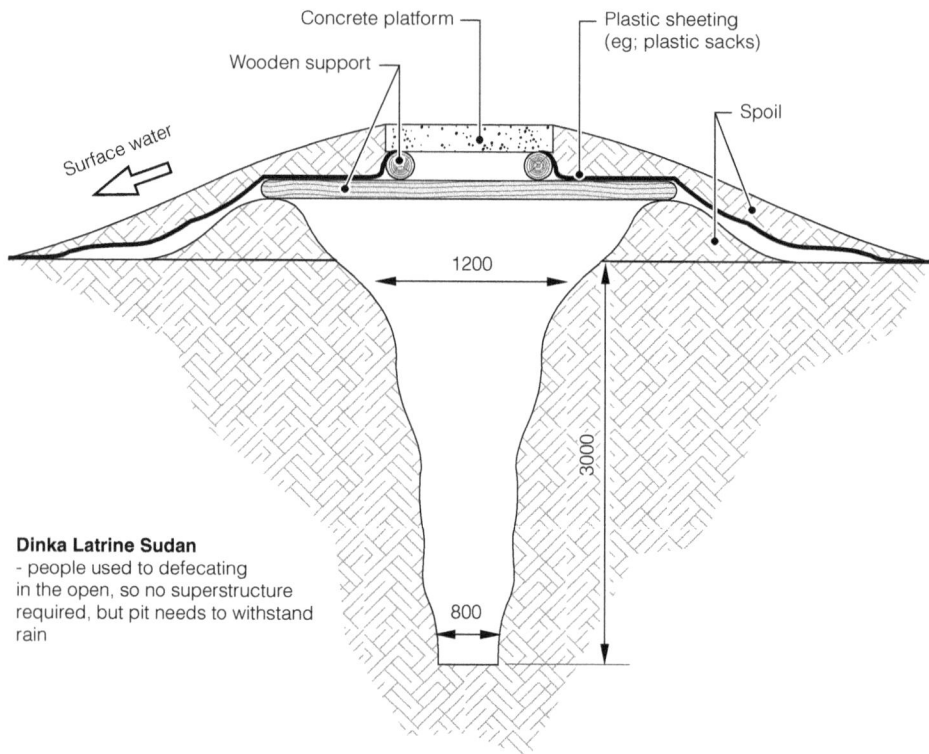

Concrete platform

Wooden support

Plastic sheeting (eg; plastic sacks)

Spoil

Surface water

1200

3000

Dinka Latrine Sudan
- people used to defecating in the open, so no superstructure required, but pit needs to withstand rain

800

* Design from Médecins sans Frontières.

Figure 6.12. Latrine designed without superstructure*

Meeting cultural demands

Many cultural, social and religious implications relate to the use of latrines. Muslim practices may dictate the direction you face in the toilet; Hindu and Chinese practices may specify where the latrine is in the house. Local customs can only be ascertained by talking to men and women. The priority placed on privacy in some Muslim and Central American societies mean women may not wish to use a toilet if there is a gap under the door that people can see under. The other extreme was some people in Southern Sudan, who did not want to enter a building to defecate, so the engineers designed the latrine shown in Figure 6.12.

In some other communities, husbands and wives are traditionally not allowed to use the same latrine, for example because to do so would make them sterile. Sometimes over a period of time, where separate latrines are not affordable or feasible, brave individuals may choose to break these traditions, and this often happens when people move to urban areas. Where a family follows these beliefs or practices, provision of separate facilities for male and female may be necessary. Sometimes neighbours may each build a latrine and designate one to be shared by the females of both families and the other by the males.

In some communities, defecation over pits is thought to make women infertile. In other communities, pregnant women are not allowed to use pit latrines. Some people do not use latrines for fear that 'sorcerers' can gain access to faeces, which they can then use for hostile purposes.

Figure 6.13. Design details can be discussed by the community

Talking about sanitation

Most engineers are men; talking about a private activity such as sanitation can be a sensitive subject, especially with groups of women. One method of focussing discussion is to draw a keyhole on a large sheet of paper and ask groups of men or women to squat over the keyhole and draw round their feet, so the slab can be designed to suit the whole community (as shown on Figure 6.13). Use the exercise to ask about other issues, such as cleaning the slab, the size and location of the superstructure or needing a handhold so pregnant or elderly people have support when they get up. Disabled people may need more space. This activity may have to be managed by a woman for women's groups and a man for men's groups, or the squat plate could be placed behind a screen.

On plot sanitation

Both on-plot and sewered sanitation systems have impacts on the household in terms of design and operation.

Having promoted sanitation to motivate people to build the household part of a sanitation scheme, engineers should know how to meet those demands. There are many options for latrine superstructures and substructures (pits, composting latrines, aqua privies etc.). The engineer can discuss these options with each householder according to the status, convenience and other benefits that each can provide — and at what cost. The size of the superstructure should meet the users' needs. Corrugated iron sheet of fixed widths or standard blockwork latrines may cause problems if they are too small for large or disabled people who require more room. The superstructures shown in Figure 6.14 are all ventilated using a pipe[52] and have no windows as a fly control measure. None of these may be suitable for children who are afraid of the dark.

Latrines for children in Sri Lanka

In Sri Lanka, child-sized latrines were installed without walls under the eaves of the houses. Normal latrines were too big and too far away and dark, especially for young girls... thus inciting a fear of falling in. This site adjustment made it easier to train the children and it promoted a more fearless use of latrines.

Mainstreaming Gender, UNICEF, 1998

---

52. VIP – Ventilated Improved Pit latrines where the superstructure is designed to promote ventilation and exclude flies.

Figure 6.14. Latrine superstructures

Figure 6.15. Do raised latrines offer privacy?

Locating the latrine where the men and women of the household want it can ensure privacy and convenience. A raised pit latrine may be needed if the groundwater table is high, but this does make it obvious when somebody is climbing up to use it (see Figure 6.15). Orientating the door away from public areas, making sure it is hidden by trees or buildings or building a screen may be an important design factor for women users. This may over-ride the need to orientate the door to catch the prevailing wind or ensure sunshine heats up the vent pipe – both technical methods of improving ventilation of the latrine. The orientation and location should conform to cultural sensibilities.

Engineers will also be aware that land availability on the family plot is a critical issue for on-plot sanitation in congested urban areas. However research has shown that this does not necessarily deter people from having a latrine.

The pit in pit latrines may become smelly and cause nitrate hazards to groundwater if the excreta are too wet. Providing separate urinals for men reduces the moisture content of the pit and reduces leachates. Urine diversion is not so simple for women.

Simple engineering solutions can also make the latrine more convenient to use, as the two figures showing overhung latrines demonstrate (Figures 6.16 and 6.17). Women and children are more likely to use a latrine if access is easy and safe.

Different people need different sizes of footrests on pedestals, so make the footrests large enough for men, women and children to use comfortably. Similarly, pedestals may need to be tapered so people can tuck their feet under the seat.

Pit latrines do need to be cleaned and managed, for example:

* Latrine slabs need to be cleaned and this job is often the responsibility of women. The engineer's responsibility is to design and build the facility so that it does not get dirty quickly and can be cleaned easily. Ensuring a smooth surface will help prevent dirt collecting and make cleaning easier. Sloping the sides of squat holes and pedestal holes away from the top stops excreta collecting on the sides of the hole. Using a keyhole shaped squat hole reduces the hole size (so children are less afraid of falling in) whilst keeping the hole suitable for urinating and excreting without missing, as shown in Figure 6.18.

Figure 6.16. Overhung latrine with poor access

Figure 6.17. Safe access to an overhung latrine

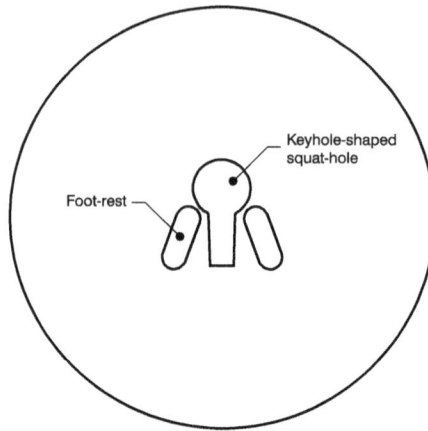

Figure 6.18. Squat hole sand pedestals

- Pour-flush latrines rely on water to work. If women are the main water collectors for a household, choosing such a technology may increase their workload and so should be discussed with them first. They may prefer pour-flush latrines, as they are more 'modern' and easier to keep clean or smell less than pit latrines. Men need to be made aware of the workload that they impose on women when they use too much water in the latrine (Figure 6.19).

- Composting latrines are a good technical option, but they require extra work to manage them. This is most likely to add to women's workload and should only be considered with their active agreement. The 'compost' exposes householders to health hazards that other latrines do not cause, but may improve nutrition through better crop production. Having a composting latrine in the house can be acceptable and allow greater privacy and access than an external latrine.

- Pit latrines have to be emptied. Men and women dispose of various items down the pit, such as condoms, plastic bags, sanitary towels[53] and children's nappies. Such objects lead to pits filling more rapidly than needed and may cause blockages when pits are emptied by suction pumps. This operation and maintenance problem can best be solved through user education, rather than trying to design an engineering solution, although the engineer may then have to address household solid waste management. There may be cultural restrictions on disposing of sanitary towel waste.

---

53. Sanitary towel waste: *Women use cloths when they are menstruating. These may be washed and re-used before eventually being disposed of, through burning, burial or down a latrine.*

Figure 6.19. Pour-flush latrine

What's hiding in the latrine?

Latrine covers can keep snakes and spiders out, as this simple design shows. The cover is fixed, so it cannot be lost or dropped down the hole. A simple mechanism such as a rope or long handle makes it easy to close with a foot, so you don't have to touch it.

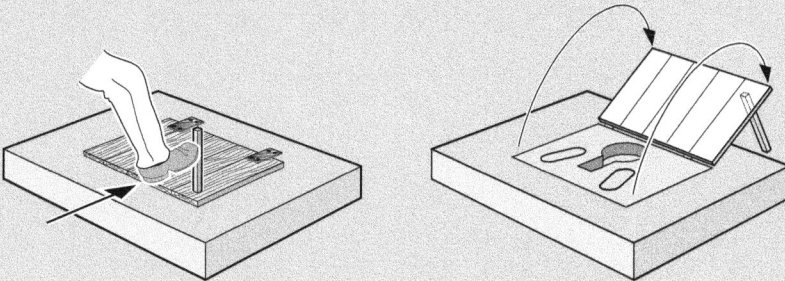

Design from Médecins sans Frontières

Sewerage and sewage treatment

Many of the issues that relate to on-plot sanitation also relate to sewerage systems, as the toilet is still located within the household area. Apart from excreta, many other objects get disposed of down sewers and some of these, such as condoms, sanitary towels and children's nappies (diapers) have clear links to either men or women. The engineer will need to be aware of this and take action accordingly. These may block pipes, especially small-bore systems or where the pipe and manhole surfaces are not smooth or pipe velocities are low. Treatment systems, such as screens and macerators, will also need to take these objects into account. Other management methods may be more appropriate, for example targeting men and women separately to encourage them to dispose of these objects in another way. Engineers may have to improve solid waste management to provide an alternative disposal route.

School sanitation

Sanitation at schools is seen as an important element of two Millennium Development Goals, the universal primary education of children by 2015 and eliminating gender disparities in primary and secondary education by 2005.

Pupils and staff regard sanitation facilities as important, and there are specific gender-related aspects to their provision.

- Providing appropriate sanitation facilities can have a major effect on the enrolment and attendance of teenage girls. Various studies have shown that one of the reasons teenage girls drop out of schools is that they or their parents consider the sanitation facilities provided there are inappropriate to meet the needs of girls that have reached puberty.

Lessons in sanitation

In an evaluation of a DPHE-DPE-UNICEF project in Bangladesh in 1994;

- The provision of water and sanitation services increased girls' attendance by 11%.
- More than 80% of students interact with their family members to discuss the practices concerning sanitation and hygiene acquired at school, resulting in higher sanitation coverage in the school catchment area compared to the district coverage.

Dipa Sen, 26th WEDC International Conference, Dhaka

- Lack of appropriate sanitation facilities for female members of staff at schools can discourage women teachers from working there. The absence of women teachers can contribute to a reduced number of girls wanting to stay on at school.

- Good sanitation at schools provides positive lessons on good hygiene and sanitation that can often be transferred to their homes. Children who have used good latrines and hand washing facilities at school are more likely to promote similar good sanitation practices in their own homes. Unfortunately if school latrines are in poor condition, this can discourage the adoption of any latrine.

Some of the design criteria that engineers should consider include:

- Provide the correct number of latrines for the proportion of boys and girls. More stalls have to be provided for girls than boys, especially if urinals are used. Providing urinals for boys allows urine to be treated separately, so reducing odours from pit latrines and reducing nitrates leaching from the pit.

- Separate blocks may have to be provided for girls and boys. Girls may prefer a physical separation of the blocks. The cleaners for each block may have to be selected according to gender considerations.

- Ensure the latrines provide privacy for the users, but are not so secluded that bullying becomes a problem.

- Provide separate hand-washing areas for teenage boys and girls. Girls may have to use the facilities for washing sanitary towels and so will want to do this in private.

- The area around the latrines should be secure, to prevent children from leaving school and prevent outsiders either using the latrines or even threatening the school children.

- Latrines for young children should not be dark and frightening. This may mean relaxing the design criteria for VIP latrines, where managing the light in the pit can make the superstructure dark.

Other communal and institutional latrines (in markets or bus stations) may have to take into account similar design factors. Like school latrines, these can only be ascertained by involving the men and women who will be using them.[54]

Sullage

Sullage or grey water is the wastewater from washing (clothes, utensils or people), food preparation and household activities. It may arise inside the home or near the water source (e.g. car washing for men, clothes washing for women). This water is dirty but is not heavily polluted with

A latrine for all market traders?

"A standard public latrine block had been built in a new market in Tanzania. It had two cubicles for men and one urinal, and two cubicles for women. Market traders and shoppers in the areas were mostly women. There were no hand washing facilities. It was a Muslim area; no water had been provided for anal cleansing and the amount of water used would impair the performance of the latrines constructed."

Paul Deverill, Consultant

---

54. The School Sanitation and Hygiene Education website has more information: http://www.irc.nl/sshe/

Figure 6.20. Getting rid of grey water is a domestic problem

faecal material (except for babies' nappies). Where excreta disposal is via a pit, separate facilities have to be provided to dispose of sullage. Because this water mostly arises from household activities, it may not be a high priority for men, but is a problem for women. Soakaways and infiltration trenches can provide low-cost options. The grey water can also be re-used for irrigation, as long as the irrigation method, crops and quality of the water are all considered together, so pollution and contamination of crops does not occur (Figure 6.21).

Sullage can also be managed by providing washing facilities (for clothes and people) at a place where water is available and where wastewater can be disposed of easily. Washing facilities for women have to balance privacy and convenience.

Figure 6.21. Wastewater for irrigation

Urban drainage[55]

Flooding of homes and pollution of watercourses resulting from poor drainage management will have greater impacts on women, who work at home, clean the house and collect water, than on men living in the same area (see Figure 6.22). Men may be more affected by the disruption to transport facilities, hindering access to employment. This is traditionally a municipal engineering issue and so needs political influence to bring about change. Engineers can work on a policy level to ensure that this problem is given a higher priority.

Drainage projects tend to concentrate on large schemes to control flooding, especially when it disrupts public life. Concentrating on domestic flooding will necessitate more attention being given to minor drainage networks rather than trunk drains. Flood proofing houses (through raising floor levels (see Figure 6.23) or placing bunds around homes) can reduce the impact of repeated minor floods.

Solid waste management

Solid waste (material that no longer has any value to the person disposing of it) is generated from both domestic and commercial sources. In low-income countries, domestic waste can constitute up to 75 per cent of the waste collected, due to the lower amounts generated by commercial activities.

---

55. *Storm Drainage, An Engineering Guide to the Low-cost Evaluation of System Performance*, Pete Kolsky, ITDG, 1999 gives guidance on ways to work with communities to measure flooding.

Figure 6.22. Flooding brings environmental issues into the home

Figure 6.23. This school is being built on raised ground to avoid the frequent floods in the area

As the bulk of the waste is domestic, the need to involve women, who dominate domestic activities, is clear. In rural areas, women manage the whole of the solid waste management cycle. They sort, re-use, recycle and dispose of the waste, often within their domestic area through burning, burial, composting or dispersal. In more densely populated urban areas, the opportunities for such activities are limited and so the waste must be disposed of outside the household area. Before it is disposed of however, it may still be sorted, re-used, recycled or sold. Promoting increased source separation, waste re-use or re-cycling may add to the domestic workload and increase the burden on women. Encouraging the reduction of waste production through the reduction in the use of plastic bags may also impact on women – they use them because they are convenient. Women in charge of domestic work control what makes up domestic waste.

The transfer of waste outside the household is a crucial activity to be considered in the management of solid waste. This transfers the work from domestic (female) control to commercial or community (male or female) control. Physically, socially and economically, the waste transfer must take into account the needs of the householder. Placing public bins may not work if they are too far away, as the time taken to transport the waste may be seen as too costly in terms of labour and time. Household collection may improve the physical movement of the waste, but needs to be balanced by the financial cost to the householder and this may be determined by

Understanding rubbish

"When I was in my late twenties, the municipal corporation arranged to send what is called a 'ghanta gaadi' (a mobile trash collection bin mounted on wheels and trundled along by an employee of the Sanitation Department), in the locality where we lived. One day in October, when I carried the trash from our home to the gaadi, the employee, who happened to be a middle-aged woman, told me not to trash any sanitary pads over the next 10 days, as it was the Navratri festival. She was worshipping the goddess and hence having to handle menstrual material would not be acceptable, she said. She had no qualms about handling any other kind of trash! After some deliberation, our family began make it a point to themselves deposit all trash in the large containers provided in each locality by the municipal corporation, thus avoiding passing on our 'dirty work' to others."

Real Life Case Study reported by Kalpavriksh, a Pune based NGO quoted in Menstrual Hygiene and Management in Developing Countries: *Taking Stock*, 2004, Sowmyaa Bharadwaj and Archana Patkar, Junction Social, Mumbai,India

who in the household pays for the service. If the needs of the (woman) householder are not met, the waste may be dumped on the street or in a drain. Disputes can arise between neighbours over the improper disposal of waste. Door to door collection of waste by scavengers allows women to sell waste they have separated at home, giving them an income.

In urban solid waste management waste is transported away from the household and goes through a variety of stages of collection, storage, reclamation and final disposal (see Figure 6.24). Collection of the waste from the household can be either formal (municipal or private) or informal. The formal sector is dominated by male employees, which may lead to problems if they have to collect waste from female householders, especially in sexually segregated societies. The formal sector is characterised by the use of machines, capital investment, authority and the largely male workforce. Where women are employed, they are more likely to be in casual rather than permanent positions.

Informal waste management can be an important way of earning a living for very poor people. They can charge to take waste away, sort it and sell the material that can be reclaimed. The informal sector is characterised by the low socio-economic status of the people working in it. They are often the old, the young, migrants, people discriminated against on racial

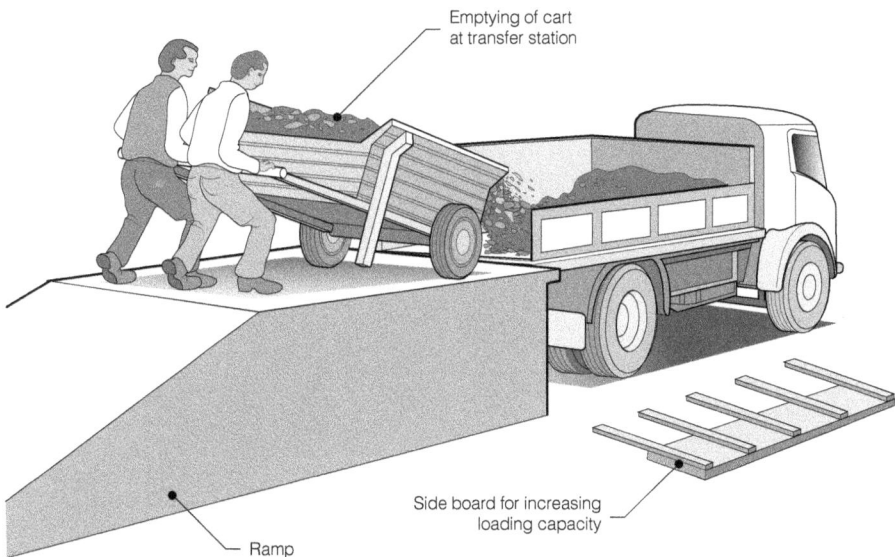

Emptying of cart at transfer station

Side board for increasing loading capacity

Ramp

Figure 6.24. A waste transfer station — a public facility

or religious grounds or people without education and skills. The key parameter seems to be culture or poverty, rather than gender. However, within this group, women are further marginalized. They often have less education, less access to credit, less access to markets and less mobility, restricting the work they can do. Where women are culturally restricted from working outside, children may take over the role of waste pickers.

Women in both the formal and informal sectors are likely to undertake 'lighter' duties, such as sweeping rather than transporting the waste. They are also more likely to be constrained from travelling far, so are involved in waste collection rather than transport, backed up by the impression that driving vehicles is men's work. Work can involve being in public places, such as bus stations, where they can be harassed, or lonely areas, such as dumps, where they may be liable to attack. Women who can only collect waste during the day and in groups have less access to items that can be reclaimed than men who can work before dawn. Even when waste is dumped at a landfill site, men will have the first option to pick over the waste.

Culturally people see waste in a variety of ways. Other people's waste is more distasteful than their own. Institutional methods of controlling dumping, such as fines, only work in a cash economy where money is valued and the fine can be enforced. Other methods of controlling dumping may be to demonstrate a communal displeasure with the people who do

Figure 6.25. Formal and informal waste management needs to be considered

not comply or to invoke religious sentiments, as people will not pollute somewhere that is held sacred with unclean rubbish.

Hygiene promotion

Providing safe water and sanitation facilities will have a greater impact on the health of a community if they are taught how to make the most of these services, in order to reduce routes for faecal-oral disease transmission. This includes the importance of washing people, food and cooking utensils, keeping latrines clean, not polluting water once it has been collected and a variety of other healthy practices. Engineers need to plan this activity into their projects and ensure that the message given to men and women can be carried out using the infrastructure provided.

Many of these hygiene activities will be the responsibility of women, so they will need to be targeted during the promotion campaign. However, there is evidence that educating children can provide peer pressure at school to ensure the messages are spread. The importance of women in maintaining hygienic practices should not mean that men are excluded from this process. They can take on some of these additional activities that hygienic behaviour requires, as well as ensuring that they keep latrines and urinals clean. Men's part of food preparation, such as harvests and butchery can also add to hygienic practices. Poor hygiene by one member of the household can still provide a route for disease to the whole household.

Washing children – how much water do you need?

A health team in Dodoma, Tanzania overcame resistance to the desirable practice of washing of children's faces more frequently by organising a demonstration with women and men. The average woman with three children had estimated that she needed three litres of water each time she washed her children's faces. The researchers organised a meeting with men and women in two separate groups. They first held up a litre can of water and asked each group how many faces they thought they could wash with the water. The women guessed five to six, the men one to two. The researchers then invited volunteers in both groups to put their guess to the test. The men managed to wash 12 faces, the women over 30. This clearly demonstrated that washing children's faces was less of a waste of water and time than thought and laid a more fertile basis for a programme to reduce trachoma incidence through improved hygiene.

McCauley et al.,1990
quoted in *Gender in Water Resources 33 E 1998*, IRC, page 122

Figure 6.26 shows that breaking the transmission of disease requires both technical and behavioural barriers. The management of different parts is traditionally shared between men and women, but needs to be co-ordinated to have the largest impact. Providing infrastructure without encouraging behaviour change will limit the effectiveness of the investment.

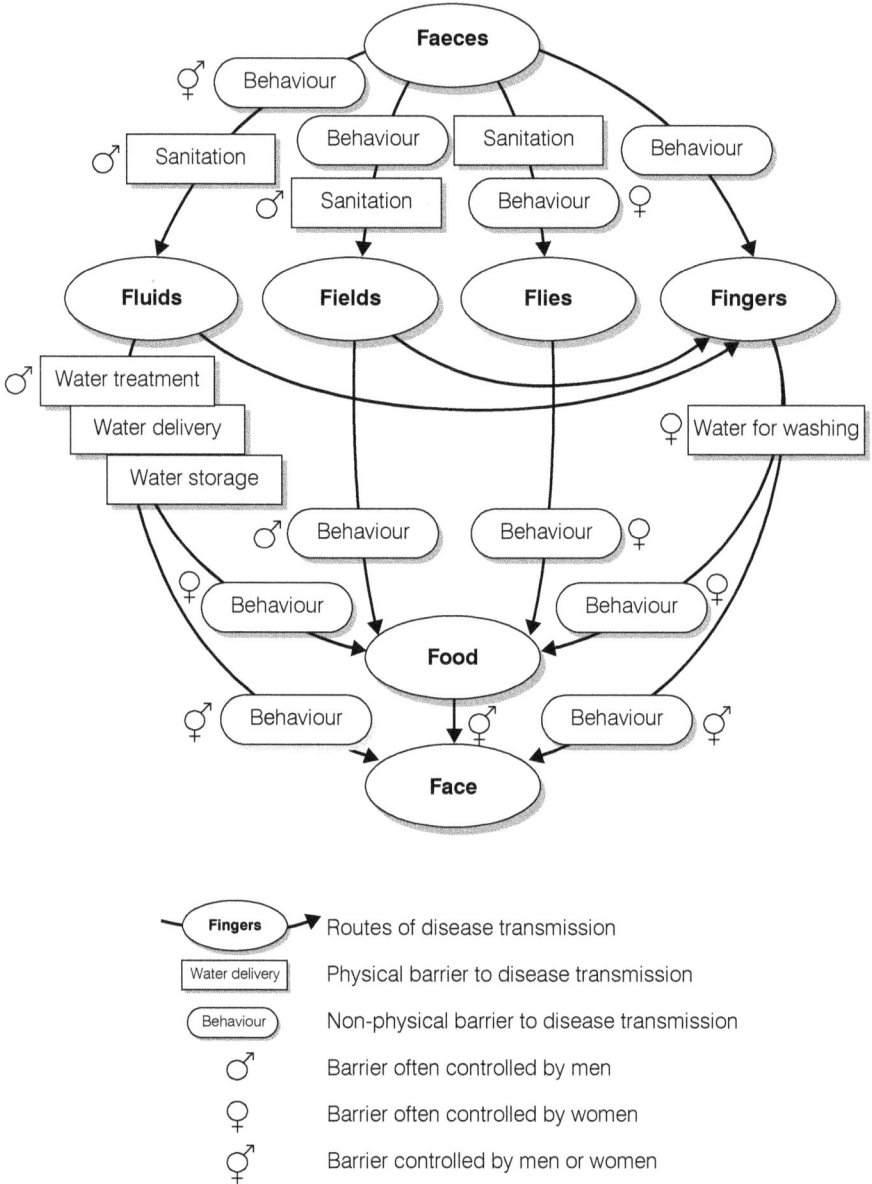

Figure 6.26. The transfer of disease from faeces to mouth

Irrigation[56]

"[In Africa] women provide the majority of the human effort which contributes to irrigated production on a day-to-day basis. In addition, the number of women who lead rural households in Sub-Saharan countries appears to be increasing.

In projects where more than three quarters of the end users are women it is not uncommon to find that women have a minimal or nominal role in planning and continue to have a minimal role in operating, managing and developing the system and in controlling their productive resources."[57]

Felicity Chancellor

Irrigation is one factor of agricultural production. Inputs of land, labour, fertilizer, seeds are also required to produce the crop. Subsequent activities of marketing, transport, food preparation and storage are necessary to translate the produce into the final outcome, which may be increased food security, increased nutrition or cash for school fees. It is this final outcome that is the indicator of a successful agricultural project. Increases in crop production are wasted if marketing, transport or labour shortages mean the final goal is not realised.

Land ownership and allocation is also a factor in agricultural production. Legal or cultural restrictions on who may own land may adversely affect women, especially female-headed households. Where land is being re-distributed, equality concerns must be actively considered. Women may prefer smaller plots closer to home, so they can integrate agricultural tasks with domestic duties, rather than larger pieces of land further away.

Irrigation is not only part of agricultural production, but can have positive and negative impacts on wider society. Pressure on water resources can mean people have to travel further to collect water for domestic use or use lower quality water. This will have an impact on women as collectors of water and carers for the sick. Women may also choose different crops than men, with different priorities in terms of marketing, food or fuel production.

---

56. For information on how make irrigation more sensitive to the needs of men and women see *Gender-Sensitive Irrigation Design — Guidance for smallholder irrigation development,* F. Chancellor, N. Haslip, D. O'Neill, H.R. Wallingford, 1999.
57. Felicity Chancellor, 'Women in Irrigation' ODA 1996.

Allocating smaller plots separately to men and women instead of allocating bigger plots to the household heads has positive production and social benefits.

- When both men and women have irrigated plots, the productivity of irrigated land and labour is higher than that in households where only men have irrigated plots.
- Women are equally good or even better irrigation farmers than men. Those who have obtained irrigated plots are proud of their increased abilities to contribute towards the needs of the households.
- Women prefer to contribute to their households by working on their own plots rather than providing additional labour to their spouse's or to collective plots.
- As women become economically less dependent upon their husbands, they can help support their family and increase their own opportunities for individual accumulation of wealth in the form of livestock.
- The effect of having an individual plot significantly improves the bargaining position of a woman within a household and is a source of pride in the household and community.

A Plot of One's Own: Gender Relations and Irrigated Land Allocation Policies in Burkina Faso, Zwarteveen, M., 1996

Labour

"...men and women often perceive themselves doing most of the work or claim to be doing the same piece of work. However, the abundance of women to be found in the field at any given time, suggests that women are likely to be doing the work they claim. Agencies and institutions traditionally regard women as helpers of men..."[58]

Felicity Chancellor

In many countries it is women who are responsible for sowing, weeding, harvesting, winnowing and often in carrying crops from the field. Introducing irrigation may mean that women's work is increased, as both the land area increases and the season is extended, requiring year-round weeding and harvesting. This has an impact on women's other jobs.

---

58. F. Chancellor, N. Haslip, D. O'Neill, *Gender-Sensitive Irrigation Design – Guidance for smallholder irrigation development,* H.R. Wallingford, 1999.

Subsistence agriculture is often women's work and its value in terms of household and national food security is widely overlooked.

Technology

External inputs cannot always be relied upon, whether it is tractor services for levelling ground or spare parts for motorised pumps. The use of simpler, cheaper technologies that can be managed by the users, such as short furrow levelling or treadle pumps (see Figure 6.27) may be preferable to using the 'best' technology. Gravity systems, whilst having greater capital costs, may have lower overall costs, especially when risk of failure is accounted for. Wealthier farmers can invest in small portable pumps, but pump failure can lead to crop failure for the poorer farmer.

Figure 6.27. A treadle pump

Levelling is an important part of land preparation. However, lack of draught or mechanical power can mean this is carried out by hand and therefore often by women. Sustained use of hand hoes can cause back problems and exhaustion. Sprinklers require less levelling, but heavy hoses may be difficult to use and demand more skill in positioning.

Timing of watering is an issue for women who have competing demands on their time. This aspect of management and design has to be discussed to ensure that availability of water is sufficiently flexible to suit women's lifestyles. This is easier on very small irrigation schemes than on large schemes with rotational delivery of water. Allocating water during the night puts female irrigators at risk of attack.

Drainage is often a neglected aspect of irrigation design, being addressed only when agricultural production begins to suffer through salinity. Poor levelling, stagnant water or failure to drain down the infrastructure periodically can lead to increased disease vectors (e.g. malaria, schistosomiasis). Using chemical controls can also have adverse health and financial impacts that can be avoided by correct design and operation.

Watering cans

Women water their vegetables laboriously with empty margarine tins or heavy buckets, often washing away the manure they had applied and breaking seedlings. They were crying for watering cans. The research team discussed alternatives with the group and it was agreed that some equipment would be bought and the women would test it recording time and perceptions of effort and efficiency of watering.

After a six-week trial, the women presented their findings: watering cans were good for seedlings but too slow for mature plants. Plastic buckets were light, cheap and durable and made for faster watering.

The women were very pleased. They were aware that the right tool made work easier, and invested their own money in some plastic buckets. The main thing that changed was their perception of themselves as judges and selectors. They soon set about finding a small two-pronged fork for use in the small beds, as an alternative to the standard broad bladed hoe.

Gender-Sensitive Irrigation Design –
Guidance for smallholder irrigation development.
F. Chancellor, N. Haslip, and D. O'Neill. H.R. Wallingford, 1999

In many examples from Africa the lower than anticipated availability of female labour has depressed the size of area cultivated, and the yields gained from irrigation schemes. For example in an irrigation system in Cameroon intra-household conflicts over control of income from rice production led to women minimising their labour contributions to the irrigated rice crop controlled by their husbands in favour of their individually controlled sorghum production. This led to negative effects on rice production.

Jones, 1983 and 1986 quoted in Zwarteveeen, 1993

Where livestock are farmed, patterns of water delivery may vary. Whereas water has to be brought to plants, livestock can be brought to the watering point. This may influence demands of men and women where farming is divided along gender lines. Small numbers of animals tended at home may be treated in a different manner from large herds and flocks.

Marketing

Poor and vulnerable women often prefer to have a lower, less uncertain income throughout the year rather than investing in potentially higher returns at less frequent intervals. They have to provide for expenditure including food and household costs, school fees and medicines. This pattern does however allow them more scope for testing markets and reacting to changing demands, provided they can access independent information on prices. Women however often have less access to agricultural advice and the credit that enables a longer term view to be taken.

Men and women have different access to markets. Men are likelier to have vehicles or cash to spend on transport whilst women have to balance time at markets with domestic duties. The demands on women's time make it less easy to meet deadlines for producing bulk crops.

Training

Although communities may regard men as more suited to maintaining pumps, this can lead to inefficiencies. Having to walk to ask a man to come and start or repair a pump can entail a wait that is wasteful and can lead to crop failure. Women may feel they do not have the time to spare to attend training, but the investment should be repaid in prompter reaction to pump failures. Patterns of male rural – urban migration and multiple marriages also make the training of female technicians a sustainable action. Women may require some additional initial training to compensate for unequal access to schooling.

Transport

In looking at the infrastructure needs of women, planners tend to concentrate on the services that directly support domestic activities, such as water supplies, food security or waste disposal. Transport is vital to the support of these domestic services, providing routes for food, spare parts and expert support. It also has a large role in commercial activities. Road design need not be dominated by the needs of a limited set of stakeholders, targeted at reducing travel times between set points (see Figure 6.28). It can enhance economic activity all along the route, if designed with local men and women in mind, even though they may not travel on the road itself. Pedestrians, cyclists, people using animal power, people using public transport and drivers all have different requirements, whether for commercial, community, domestic or personal reasons.

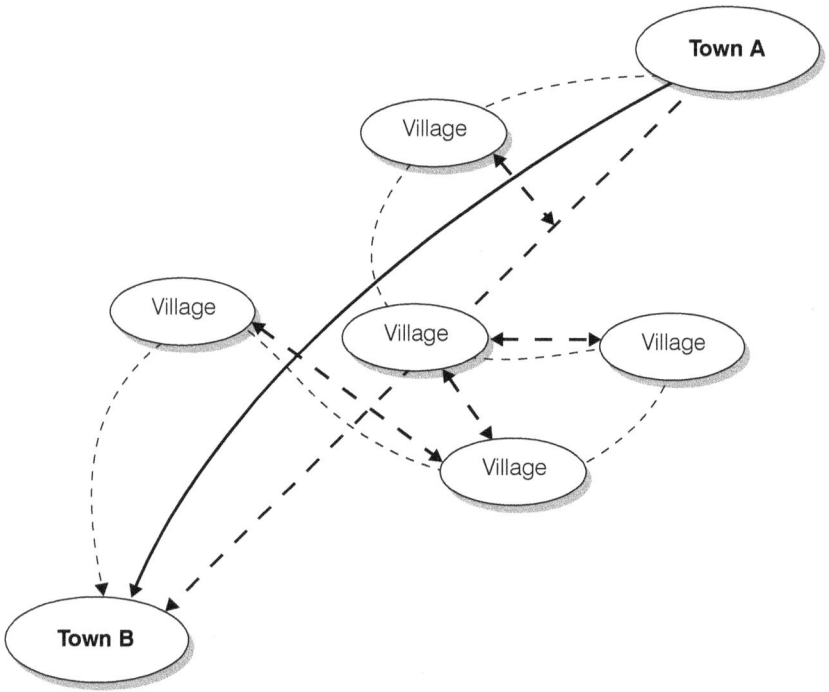

Figure 6.28. What is best route from A to B?

Reducing the walking distance to school increases attendance by girls. Increasing the access to health care reduces the time women have to spend looking after sick members of the family. Fast access to health clinics is vital during complications in childbirth.

Details of road design can also contribute to pedestrian safety. Attention to sightlines, traffic calming and the location of existing paths can reduce accidents between vehicles and pedestrians. Placing road cuttings across existing paths will inconvenience the local population. Open drains need to be provided with frequent cross points, in places where people want them (see Figure 6.29). Good road design can also lead to increased personal safety, by designing out dark corners rather than trying to provide lighting that needs to be managed and maintained.

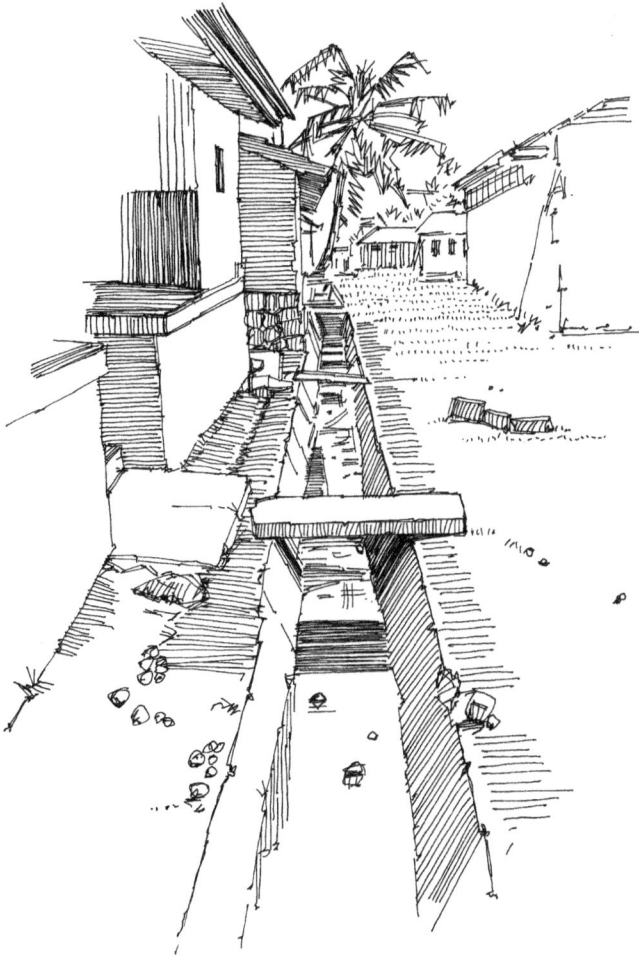

Figure 6.29. Drainage ditch with pedestrian crossings

In several cases, poor people in urban areas, though actually poorer than those in comparable rural areas, are viewed as less poor because they have access to infrastructure and basic services (Guatemala 1997b; India 1997a). Similarly, a report from India states, "Even the poorer families living in the prosperous villages are comparatively better than poor people living in medium and poorest villages, in terms of social and educational awareness, because these facilities are more accessible to them" (India 1997a).

Community poverty is related to infrastructure and service provision. In a poor rural community surveyed in Nigeria, respondents claim that every inhabitant is poor precisely because the community lacks basics such as water, electricity, roads, schoolteachers, and more (Nigeria 1995). In Uganda, a distinction is made between individual and community poverty, in which community-level poverty is defined as "a lack of key infrastructure for the entire community, for example, school, roads" and lack of security or harmony (Uganda 1998). Similarly, nearly half of the suggestions from poor Ecuadorian families about how to alleviate poverty concerned the provision of basic infrastructure (Ecuador 1996a).

The absence, or poor condition, of infrastructure, especially of feeder roads and bridges, is widespread. In many reports the poorest communities are identified as those most isolated and located farthest from roads and other key infrastructure (India 1997a; Yemen 1999; Bangladesh 1996; Mexico 1995; Guatemala 1997b; Uganda 1998; Ecuador 1996a; Ecuador 1996b; Cameroon 1995). In India, many of the poorest villages are located 15-20 kilometres from the nearest infrastructure; during the rainy season villagers find themselves completely isolated from the more developed areas. "The result is that the members of the unconnected villages remain effectively marginalized from virtually all educational institutions above primary level, from adequate health care facilities, and from important governmental and non-governmental institutions" (India 1997a). Respondents in Bangladesh (1996) and Ghana (1995b) also identify the lack of adequate roads, particularly during rainy seasons, as a key problem.

In addition to isolating communities from other infrastructure, lack of roads can also deny communities political access. Ugandan government officials who are posted in isolated areas perceive it as a kind of punishment (Uganda 1998). Similarly, the Kenya PPA [Participatory Poverty Assessment] indicates that district leaders tend to avoid villages that are only accessible through bad or dangerous roads. If they go to remote villages at all, it is only for short visits, so there is no time to witness problems directly and talk things over with stakeholders (Kenya 1996).

....continued

In addition, poor roads greatly limit inter-village and rural-urban trade (India 1997a; Ecuador 1996a). In Cameroon for instance, 86 percent of respondents in the South West Province believe that poor transportation infrastructure is a major factor in their inability to increase agricultural productivity and marketing activities (Cameroon, 1995). In Uganda, poor people report that "it is because of poor roads that the produce of the farmers is bought at low prices" (Uganda 1998).

Poor transportation infrastructure also compounds problems with obtaining service provisions such as health care and education. Two-thirds of respondents in Mexico City complain of the poor quality and lack of access to health clinics, and this problem increases in rural areas. In one rural region, Zacatecas, the average cost for transportation to the nearest doctor was $41, or the equivalent of a month's wages from the only wage labour in the area, hemp weaving. "In Zacatecas it is not rare to hear of families that have lost all of their animals and gone into debts of from 2,000 to 5,000 pesos [$365 to $900] due to sickness of a family member" (Mexico 1995). Similar problems exist in Yemen, where "poor families from remote areas go to health facilities only when in extreme need" (Yemen 1999).

Lack of transportation also affects children. Rural children in Cameroon often do not attend school because schools are located beyond walking distance, and teachers avoid working in the more isolated areas (Cameroon 1995). In Thailand, some parents remove their children from school because the combined costs of education and transportation are unaffordable (Thailand 1998). In one of the South African villages, the costs associated with transporting children to school are identified as a cause of poverty (South Africa 1998).

Narayan, Deepa with Raj Patel, Kai Schafft, Anne Rademacher and Sarah Koch-Schulte. 2000. *Voices of the Poor: Can Anyone Hear Us?* New York, N.Y.: Published for the World Bank, Oxford University Press

Emergencies

Refugees and displaced people

Women and children are often in the majority in refugee populations – with around 70 per cent of displaced people being female. This makes ensuring that the design of engineered services meets their needs extremely important. Many cultural norms are disrupted and so both the refugees and those trying to meet their needs have to adjust their preconceptions. The stereotyped male-headed household will not hold in the majority of cases. Employing only men in infrastructure projects, for food, payment or on a voluntary basis will exclude women and their dependants from the benefits that employment can bring. All people will be increasingly vulnerable.

Men at risk

Many young Sudanese men walked long distances to West Ethiopia to avoid conscription into the army. When they arrived, they were in very bad health. They were given food but morbidity and mortality rates remained high, as they did not know how to prepare food due to their normal gender roles. Then a teaching programme was implemented using the ten per cent of the refugee population who were women to teach the men how to cook so they could eat.

Understanding the Disaster Development Continuum, M. Anderson
in *Women and Emergencies*, Editor B. Walker, Oxfam 1994

Figure 6.30. Where open defecation has to be practised, privacy and safety should be considered

The engineers who had set up the water system for a camp for Burmese refugees in Bangladesh were confused that the water tanks and systems set up in the camps did not seem to be used. No one was using them, but the water level in the tanks was going down on a daily basis. One night they stayed up, hiding themselves away, and what they saw was that the women of the camp, who were Muslim and living in Purdah* were collecting water in the night by darkness so as not to be seen. The Oxfam engineers therefore changed the hours of availability of water to suit the women's cultural needs.

Gary Campbell, seconded to Oxfam from VSO

* Purdah: a cultural practice of women remaining secluded.

Security

The disruptions that have caused people to flee and the lack of social constraints within camps can expose women to increased risks of assault and rape. Siting of water supplies and sanitation facilities will need to consider this aspect carefully. Men also have increased physical risks, from the political fighting that can continue within the camp, although this will need to be addressed in a different manner than the siting of infrastructure.

Social resources

Displaced people will have lost many of their financial and physical resources; maintaining their social links can be important. Camp design and layout can influence the way people from the same community can stay together.

Menstruation does not stop just because there is an emergency. Besides the practical issues of obtaining, washing and disposing of sanitary towels, women may have cultural issues to deal with. In some societies, women have to go somewhere private whilst they are menstruating. If the whole household is living in a single room or tent, this can be very difficult.

Paul Sherlock, OXFAM

Housing needs

A Red Cross housing programme cum refugee camp established in Croatia in 1993 set out to meet some of the more developmental aspects of relief in its programming.

Family structure is one of the greatest resources for survival, yet it is the one that is often destroyed in refugee situations. When these settlements were being built, it was clear that there were several types of family structure. For example, in some families the father was present and family structure was intact. In others, where the fathers were absent, a larger group of women and children from the same village wished to stay together. Therefore, this project attempted to adapt buildings to accommodate variations in family houses to accommodate single families with 5 to 8 people, and larger houses accommodating up to 20 people. The project particularly tried to avoid mass accommodation. This fact was one of the aspects which refugees appreciated most, as they said "we can go behind our own door and lock it". However, the total amount of space per inhabitant was kept low at 3 to 5 sq.m.

Developmental Relief, Margareta Wahlstrom, IFRC Geneva, 1997

Emergency shelters

Bangladesh experienced a cyclone in May 1997 and there is currently a Federation-supported programme providing food and shelter assistance to the affected population. Local culture means there are very clear gender differences, which bring up a number of gender issues in disaster management. These include:

need for separate space for men and women in cyclone shelters to ensure women will use them during a cyclone;

need for health-workers of both sexes to ensure healthcare is truly accessible; and

awareness of men's predominance in household decision making and women's responsibilities for property, mean that women often do not move to shelters until the last warnings are heard.

Dealing with Diversity, Teresa Hanley, British Red Cross, 1997

Disaster preparedness

Emergencies do not just concern displaced people. Infrastructure has to cope with local disasters, such as flooding, adverse weather, earthquakes, as well as conflict. Vulnerable people face bigger threats because they live in areas that may be at greater risk in natural disasters, live in poorer quality housing and have a lower priority in receiving assistance from relief services due to political influence.

Women's voices will be difficult to hear in the emergency stage of a crisis. They may not be willing to leave families to attend formal meetings. Meeting women in more informal situations, such as at clinics, in queues for water or in their own home may enable their concerns to be heard.

7

Men and women in the workplace

So far, this book has concentrated on ways in which individual engineers can seek to promote gender equity and social inclusion in the infrastructure projects that they are involved with. The extent to which an engineer can steer a project or programme in favourable directions is affected by his or her own attitudes and enthusiasm. It can be substantially enhanced by a supportive working environment in the engineering organisation, whether that organisation is a national or local government department, a consultant, a contractor or an NGO.

In Chapter 7, we look at how inclusion can be fostered in the workplace and how a visibly inclusive engineering organisation can become an example for other stakeholders. Recruitment and training are crucial too. To work effectively on participatory projects, today's engineers need knowledge and experience of social and cultural issues to complement their technical skills. Key points in Chapter 7 include:

- Practise what you preach. Guidance on gender sensitive approaches and participatory processes will be better received if delivered by an organisation that is itself diverse and consultative. A diverse workforce can also make an organization more efficient and effective.

- Do not just preach. Participation is a two-way process in which the engineer and his/her organisation must expect to learn as well as teach. Practising social inclusion in the office can support participation in the field.

- Obtaining a gender balance does not mean encouraging women to do 'men's work'. It means employing men and women for their individual talents and strengths, rewarding them accordingly and adopting working practices that do not penalise either sex.

Hopefully, the previous chapters have shown that involving women and men in the different stages of infrastructure development has clear benefits in producing equitable and sustainable services for the public. Looking at how men and women engineers are managed at work can also have positive benefits both for the organisation and for the people it is serving. Although many organisations may present themselves as having neutral working practices, men and women have different experiences at work. Biases are often found in:

- recruitment and selection procedures;
- practical work conditions (working hours, office location);
- informal communication pathways;
- career development and progression; and perhaps above all in
- attitudes[59].

For example, in some situations the actual work that a woman engineer is expected to do is different from that of her male counterpart. She may be given less site work or less management involvement in contracts where adversarial approaches are favoured. There are a number of explanations for these biases and differences, some of which are examined in this chapter.

These guidelines began by examining what civil engineering is for, or rather *whom* it is for. A similar exercise can be taken for organizations that employ engineers to establish where the biases are, what effect they are having on the performance of the institution and how each might be addressed.

Acknowledging that gender biases occur in the workplace, and doing something about them, is a major step forward for a manager. A greater step is to acknowledge that if the (public) service sector in high- and low-income countries is to be sustainable, then the working practices of *all employees* face major changes. Running sustainable programmes by changing from a provision-driven to a service-centred approach means that the organisation's focus will have to adapt and people's roles will alter. Accepting this, the manager can then consider what are the best working practices for a *diverse* workforce: men, women, older, younger, skilled, semi-skilled, ethnically and socially different.

---

59. Mullins L.J., (1999) *Management and Organisational Behaviour*, Prentice Hall.

"I went to engineering school and learned how to design water systems; if I am now told to go spend the day talking to villagers who do not know what I know, I feel very frustrated. I would rather spend my time in front of my drawing board; otherwise what is the use of my engineering degree?"

Young engineer in Public Health Engineering Department,
Pakistan, quoted by Narayan, 1995

Why are we at work?

People go to work for a variety of reasons. Employees arrive at work with their own needs and expectations, some of which are tangible; salary, a vehicle, a house, allowances, job security or a computer. Some are less so, for example needing a sense of challenge, receiving appreciation, the opportunity to use one's ability, having the time to review the daily newspaper and the reward of spending large amounts of time with colleagues. What people get out of work varies from person to person, year to year, or day to day. Very often, so long as the job is being done, and unless there is an industrial dispute or complaint, managers simply do not really know how their employees feel about being at work. Yet many people at work face frustration because their individual needs and expectations are not being adequately identified or met. This results in a change in behaviour or attitude that at the very least affects individual performance but may also affect the way other people perceive their environment. Whether visible or hidden, serious or trivial, dissatisfaction at work is usually not good for business.

Why and how is work changing?

An institution providing a public service, for example water or power, has to recover costs if the service offered, the staffing levels and the institution are to be sustainable. Public services are an economic as well as a social good. Decentralization, public sector reform, commercialization and customer centred and demand driven approaches are an increasing reality. This means that the managers of public service institutions, often themselves engineers, will have specific objectives and resources to try and meet these new goals effectively. Placing greater emphasis on commercial approaches, demand responsiveness and community management requires investment and expertise beyond traditional financial and physical resource management and includes the effective management of human capital – the workforce. The provision of sustainable infrastructure services, even with capital investment and the best technological support is only as good as the productivity of the staff involved in 'making it happen'.

Efficiency and effectiveness

Staff costs are often the greatest item of expenditure in any organisation, so recruiting, retaining and motivating quality staff should be an important aim of the manager. However, crisis management and external demands result in the management of people taking a back seat. Many managers lack formal management training and because of this can attempt their new role without thinking about the different skills and approaches required of them. Often they are task focused rather than people focused. Management complacency with regard to ongoing staff motivation and productivity also leads to problems, for example in some government departments the lack of redundancy policies can serve to undermine the institution's goals.

Recruiting and, where it exists, training staff is a significant investment for an organization. Recruiting staff will be more productive if the potential pool of applicants is not restricted unnecessarily or artificially. For example, if new employees are only selected from one university, the choice will be restricted compared to recruiting from several universities of the same standard. This would also reduce the range of perspectives and experience that the new employees bring to the organization.

Retaining staff, especially as they become more experienced, is an economic imperative as the investment spent on universal education, recruitment and training has to be recouped. Denying people appropriate career paths, imposing working conditions that conflict with their life outside the workplace or failing to make adequate provision for fringe benefits can force them to look for alternative employment. It can therefore be more efficient to adapt working practices to suit the workforce rather

Staff implement polices

… to encourage each staff member and staff of implementing partners to ensure that the integration of refugee women's resources/needs takes place in his/her area of competence.

From UNHCR Policy on Refugee Women

than expecting the workforce to conform to restrictive practices that may reduce their effectiveness and commitment or force them to leave. One indicator of good personnel management and efficient productivity is low staff turnover.

Government reform and the involvement of the private sector in public service delivery and infrastructure management is presenting new challenges to traditionally managed institutions affecting the culture, working practices, transparency and decision making processes. Flatter organisations are emerging where teamwork is required. Effective teamwork and the motivation of individual staff go hand in hand.

Practising what you preach

If infrastructure service organizations aim to serve the population using community participation, consultation and transparency in decision-making, they will have more authority if the same principles of involvement are used internally. Employee participation not only enhances the status of community participation, the contribution from women and a customer-based approach within the organization, it also provides practical internal experience of such activities that can help their application externally.

The private sector has long since understood the benefit of employee involvement. Drawing more people in to decision-making roles and teamwork releases the potential of staff and encourages innovation. However, an obstacle to employee participation is the fact that an organisation's culture, its rules, conditions of service and management behaviour, can be very difficult (though not impossible) to change. People generally feel comfortable with the status quo — 'the way things are done around here'. Change rarely happens quickly and a prerequisite is that senior management must lead and manage the process with the buy-in of middle managers and trade unions. This process of change is similar to the promotion of gender equity in wider society, with both the socially excluded and the decision-makers altering their perspectives.

Who is the workforce?

Who constitutes the workforce also has significant bearing on the way an organisation responds to the demand of its customers. This is not just a matter of skill but also gender. Although female engineers do not necessarily have any greater gender awareness than their male colleagues,

Change management

"Water and sanitation services are deteriorating and the resource gap is widening, necessitating a need for undertaking reforms in this sector. A pre-requisite for successful implementation of reforms in this sector is the strengthening of the capacity of municipalities and water utilities for undertaking and implementing reforms."

S K Singh, IAS, Director (UD),
Ministry of Urban Development and Poverty Alleviation, Government of India

Employment polices

"Impartiality; RedR makes no discrimination as to nationality, race, religious belief, gender, class or political opinions. It endeavours to provide suitable personnel being guided solely by the needs of each situation."

REDR (Register of Engineers for Disaster Relief)
fundamental principle number 3

having a workforce that reflects the community profile can bring insights to the organisation. It can challenge the status quo and some assumptions, although this is not automatic. Outside the organisation, its customers will be better able to identify with staff that are not just drawn from a narrow social group. Effective organisations are increasingly aware of the necessity and value of inclusive employment strategies.

What must be in place?

Organisations do not tend to undertake change for the sake of change. There have to be stimuli, like the need to commercialize, become more demand responsive, remain competitive or implement new legislation or

---

External and internal policies

Department of Water Affairs and Forestry Gender Policy 1997
Goals for External Gender Policy

In the provision of all services and programmes in Water Affairs and Forestry, the main goals are to:

- Identify all relevant gender issues, so that all projects and programmes recognise and address issues of gender difference and inequality;
- Identify and take into account the different gender roles of women and men in a community affected by services and programmes;
- Ensure equal participation and involvement of women and men in decision-making on all projects undertaken by the Department; and
- Put a priority focus on improving the material position and status of women who have borne and still continue to bear, the brunt of past inequities.

Goals for Internal Gender Policy

Within the internal affairs of the Department, the main gender goals are to:

- Work towards gender parity in numbers at all levels of management and specialisation;
- Introduce administrative procedures to ensure that there is no discrimination against women in recruitment, placement, promotions and conditions of service; and
- Introduce all necessary measures and facilities to provide for the different biological and gender roles of both men and women.

Department of Water Affairs and Forestry, South Africa.

---

policy. The environment in which the organisation operates also has to be ready for change. Putting an enabling environment in place involves policy, legislation, rights and attitudinal change.

Policy
Many organizations have a policy on equal opportunities or gender, though some do not. The policy may be a response to legislation, a requirement of clients or an internal decision. Having a policy document is not enough, it must be made public to staff and customers, put into practice and provided with resources and the organization needs to demonstrate that it is being addressed.

Rights and legislation
At a fundamental level, even if there were not pragmatic arguments for including all members of society, or if such practices were not a matter of policy, there are still reasons for inclusive action at work. Equity and rights are strong moral arguments for ensuring the workplace is inclusive.

Just as there are laws and international agreements covering the rights of men and women in the delivery of infrastructure, there are laws covering employment rights.

Attitudinal change
All levels of the organization have to be prepared to accept or share decision-making. This requires positive attitudes to change. It can take years to move from raising awareness to initiating action and finally achieving results. The pace of change has to be matched with the readiness

of the people to alter established practices. Organizational policies have to move from addressing negative problems, such as sexual harassment and low status, to positive actions.

What can be done in the organisation?

Analysing the organization

If one of the goals of a manager is to have an inclusive, equitable organization, some indicators of equality of opportunity need to be established. Figure 7.1 shows that this is not a case of good or bad, but a continuum of possible positions. There are other targets too, such as financial status, productivity and efficiency. Human resource parameters, such as staff turnover and staff satisfaction are important indicators of the efficiency of an organization, especially government offices or consultancies where most of the financial resources are invested in staff[60].

Gender expertise may be useful, but

> ... very few gender experts have experience or training in management and organizational development in the traditional sense... This means [gender experts] may not have tools to address the problem which will necessarily be understood or accepted by those who are part of the problem.[61]

Identifying indicators

As with any social analysis, a variety of indicators could be used to see if an organization is inclusive. Gender and economic status are two simple measures, but others may be more important in specific contexts. For example, in the UK, the police service is under pressure to recruit people from a range of ethnic backgrounds in order to reflect the constitution of society in general.

An analysis by gender (or other suitable measure) needs to be assessed in context. Very rarely will the balance between men and women doing a particular job at a particular seniority be 50:50. The ratio of female to male graduates in engineering is normally low (e.g. 10:90). This proportion reduces with experience, due to low numbers of female students in the past, girls' access to primary and secondary education, and women leaving

---

60. A useful starting point for analysing gender issues within an organisation is the Gender Scan tool prepared by Streams of Knowledge: www.streamsofknowledge.net/toolbox4.html
61. Macdonald M, Sprenger E and Dubel I., *Gender and Organizational Change: Bridging the Gap Between Policy and Practice*, p107, Royal Tropical Institute, The Netherlands, 1997.

the profession. Having one or two women in positions of power is not necessarily a sign of equity. About 30 percent of each layer of the workforce in any organisation needs to be female before parity of opportunity can be assumed[62].

Having one or two women or people of a different social group may have two effects[63].

- The majority (e.g. men) react more strongly as a group, with shared jokes, experiences and language that force the woman to be excluded or join in.

- The woman can also take on a variety of roles:

  - becoming "better" than the majority and more masculine than the men;

  - becoming invisible, doing nothing so as not to attract attention; or

  - becoming more radical than normal.

---

62. ibid.
63. ibid.

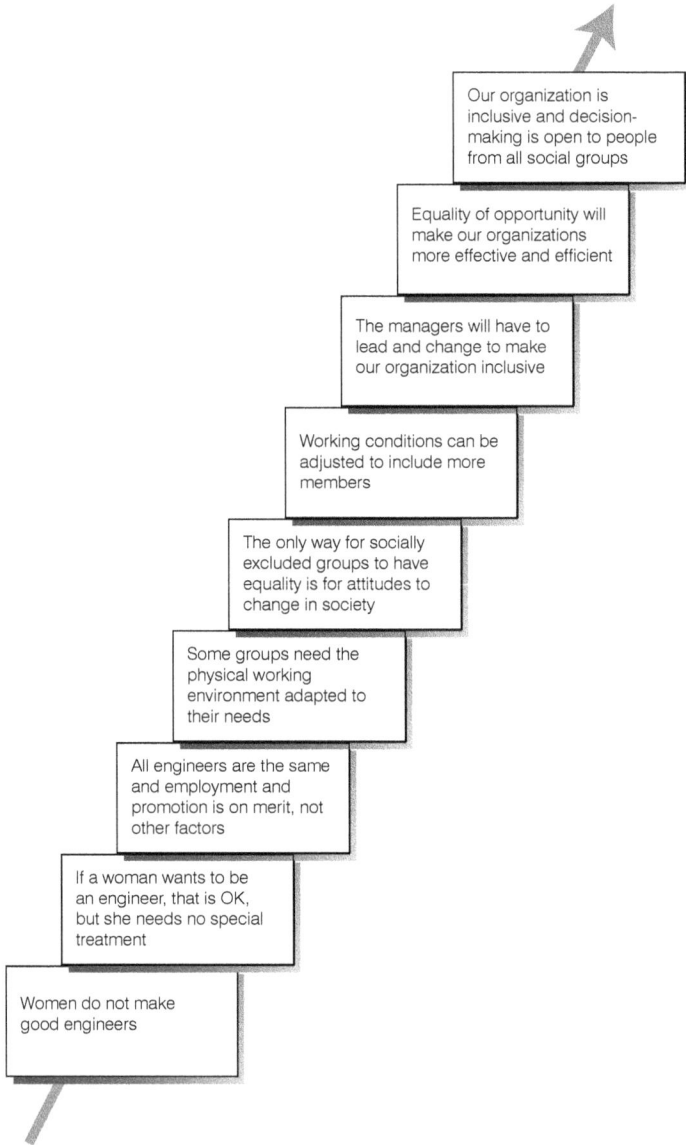

Figure 7.1. Continuum of attitudes to change

The boxes, from bottom to top, read:

- Women do not make good engineers
- If a woman wants to be an engineer, that is OK, but she needs no special treatment
- All engineers are the same and employment and promotion is on merit, not other factors
- Some groups need the physical working environment adapted to their needs
- The only way for socially excluded groups to have equality is for attitudes to change in society
- Working conditions can be adjusted to include more members
- The managers will have to lead and change to make our organization inclusive
- Equality of opportunity will make our organizations more effective and efficient
- Our organization is inclusive and decision-making is open to people from all social groups

Organization structure — what is and is not seen

Managers who are interested in addressing issues of inclusiveness can start by assessing management structure. As well as an official system of hierarchies and relationships (who is managing whom and how the system can be by-passed), different people within the organisation will usually perceive power relations from their own perspective. Asking employees

Site visits

During the initial stages of a recent water supply project, it was necessary for the engineer to go to the field to enter into dialogue with the community regarding the design and location of the supply. The engineer in question is a woman. The woman discussed with her husband the fact that the site was some distance away and therefore would require an overnight stay. Though concerned for her safety, he agreed that she should go, it was an important aspect of her professional work and he supported her. He and his wife felt much better about the trip because a second engineer, male and a distant relative of the couple was also able to make the journey. The work in the field was accomplished and everything went well. However once back in the office the rumours started. Office chattering led to an uncomfortable atmosphere and the woman engineer felt hurt and mistreated by her colleagues, male and female. As a consequence, she decided that the effort of going to the field was not worth the anguish. She has remained in the office ever since.

Sue Coates and Archana Patkar. Workshop in Mumbai, 2000

from across the organization to draw up a diagram (as in Figure 7.2) of how it works will help managers to discover the different perspectives.

By drawing organizational structures from the perspective of different employees and assessing each level and discipline, an assessment can be made of the social make-up of the organization. Data can then be collated on the equality of opportunity of people reaching each level. If the main route for career development is through promotion, then the social mix of each layer in an equitable organization should reflect the layer beneath.

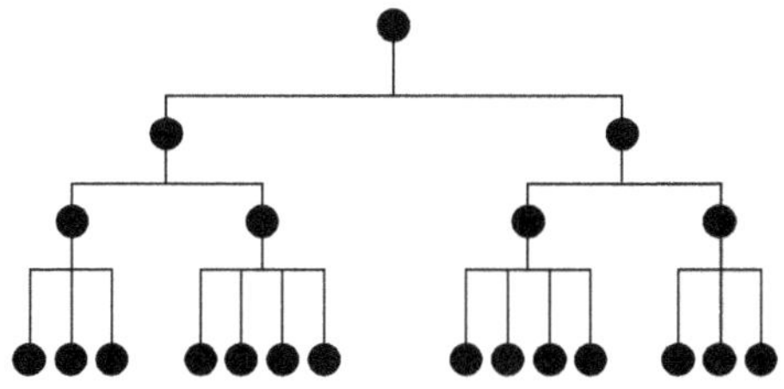

Figure 7.2. Organization chart of a workforce

Three NGOs worked in a refugee camp; one provided education, one income-generation and one sanitation, water and shelter. All had standard hierarchical organizational structures, although the educational NGO had a very flat hierarchy and considerable involvement by the refugees. The infrastructure engineering group had the most layers of management.

The employees were asked their views of the management structures. Three different models emerged.

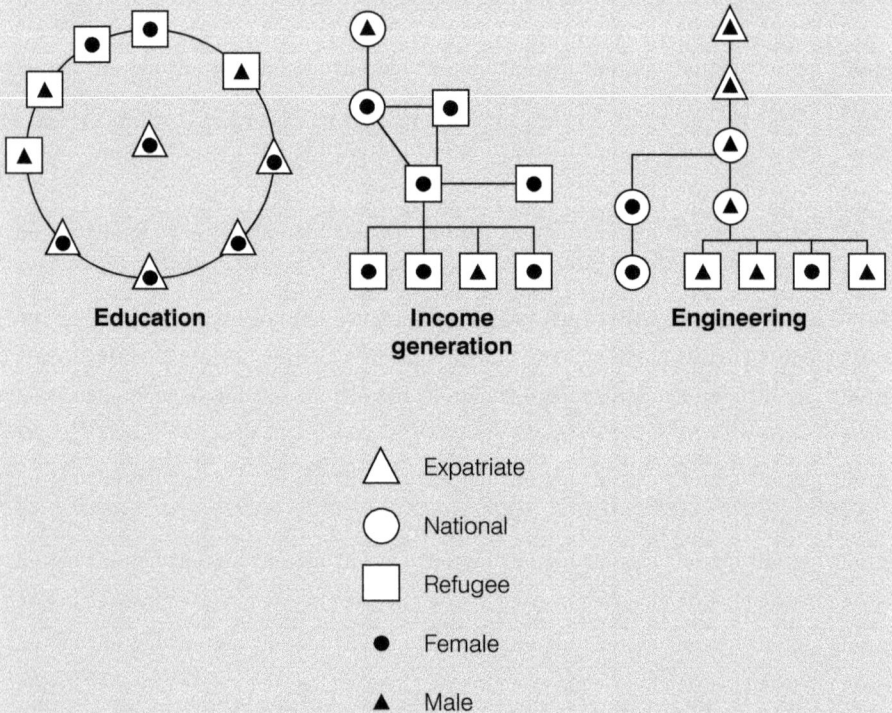

Education   **Income generation**   **Engineering**

△ Expatriate

○ National

□ Refugee

● Female

▲ Male

Community workers in the engineering organization were separate from the main work and had little impact on the work of the NGO.

From Gender, Participation and Institutional Organization
in Bhutanese Refugee Camps, Greene-Roesel and Hinton,
in *The Myth of Community* (eds Guijt and Shah) IT Publications

If the main route is through external appointments, then the social mix should reflect the mix of applicants, which in turn can be compared with the industry at large.

However, not everything can be identified in such a tangible way. Managers also must find ways to get beneath the surface of what is happening. Issues such as harassment may be unreported, assumptions unchallenged and communication routes hidden, see Figure 7.3.

Status symbols

The workforce is not just made up of social groups, but individuals. It is also useful to assess indicators of individuals. Pay is an obvious and simple measure. Most women will be paid less than their male counterparts for equal work. In the UK, 25 years after legislation for equal pay, women's salaries are 18 percent less than men, once other factors such as education and experience have been allowed for. In an engineering organization,

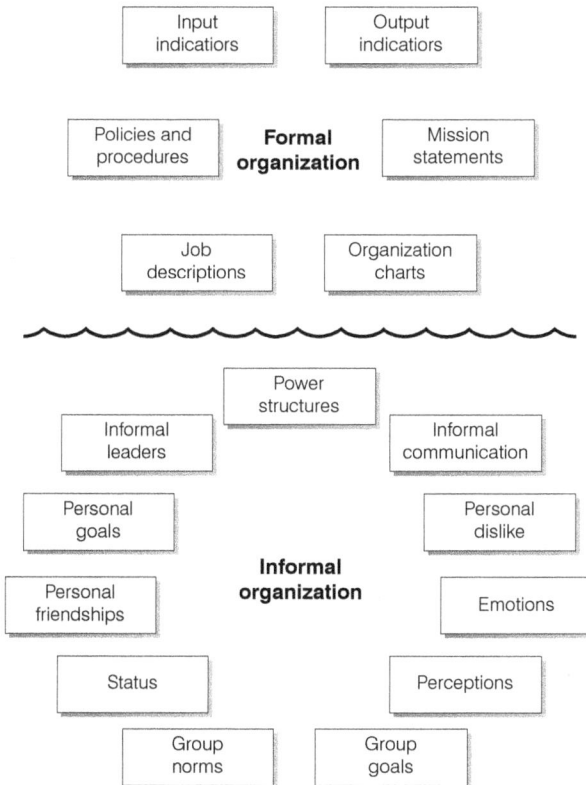

Figure 7.3. What is beneath the surface?

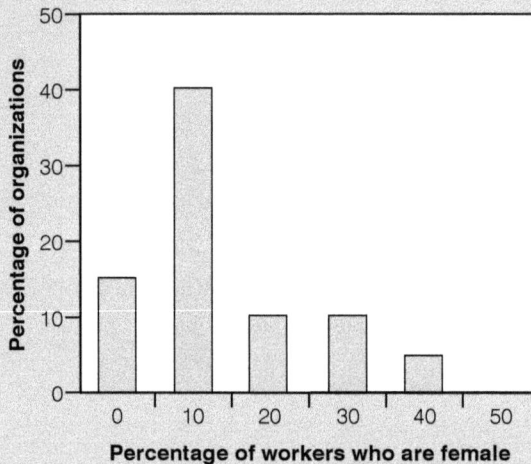
women are more likely to be employed in non-engineering fields (e.g. environment, economics). Disparity in pay may also be due to a lack of recognition that these areas of expertise are equal to engineering ones or to difficulties in providing equivalent measures of performance.

Pay is not the only benefit. Access to transport facilities (e.g. project vehicles, housing, training and career opportunities) can all be skewed away from women or other disadvantaged groups. They can also be skewed towards more advantaged groups by favouring people who share a common interest. This can change the balance of opportunity.

Other indicators may be looked at. Do sickness levels and stress rates vary between layers in the hierarchy and between social groups? Does the ability to take part in social activities vary? Can all staff take advantage of professional development activities such as evening classes or attending professional meetings?

Unequal opportunities

Poor women do not just encounter disparities in working conditions; they have to gain the necessary qualifications and experience to secure employment. Barriers can include lack of access to education at every level, expectations of family and society, lack of encouragement and role models from an early age.

Outside the workplace

When working with a community, the project officers may only be concerned with water supply or irrigation, but the local community will have a range of concerns that are not limited to development sectors. The same is true of the workplace. The different categories of work, such as domestic activities and commercial work were described earlier. Similar choices over work priorities will face the workforce. Women (due to culture) and single people are more likely to have more domestic tasks to carry out than a married male professional. High status community work, such as being a councillor or membership of professional bodies is more likely to be carried out by somebody with few domestic responsibilities. Divisions between the domestic, commercial and community work depend on the cultural context.

Who is in the organization?

In a water sector reform process, the Programme Co-ordination Unit had a committee of 11 men and one woman. The chairperson was male.

The Water Sector Development Group had a male head and female assistant. The core team was all men and the support team had three women and nine men.

The Community Management and Monitoring Unit had a male leader and female deputy, a core team of three men and three women and a support team of four women and seven men.

The Training Team had a male co-ordinator, two male and two female facilitators and four men and two women in the support team.

Nationally, only 38 per cent of girls enrolled in the last year of secondary school and only eight per cent of the university graduates in science and engineering were women.

WASHE and Gender, CMMU, Zambia 1996

Women may have different motives for becoming civil engineers than men. They also have different barriers preventing them from progressing up the career ladder. The two timelines show the factors that influence women to join or leave the profession. One is based on low and middle-income countries and one from the UK.

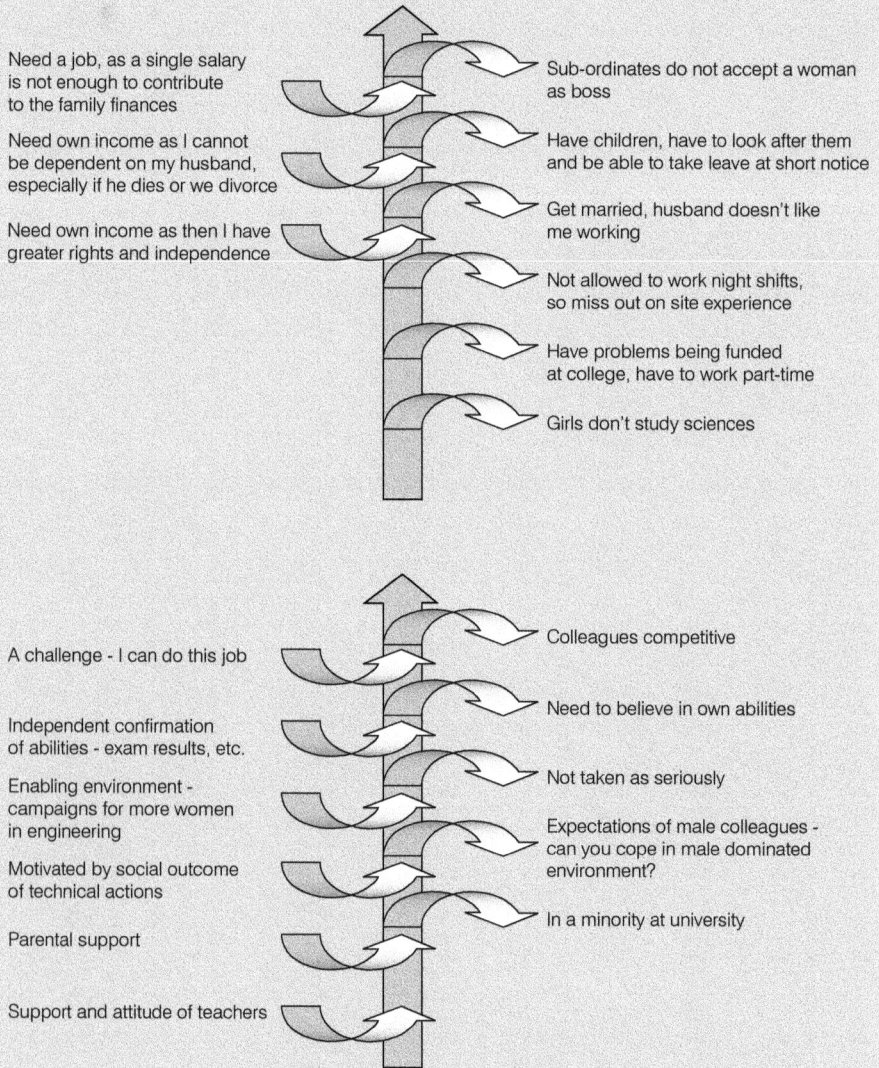

Need a job, as a single salary is not enough to contribute to the family finances

Need own income as I cannot be dependent on my husband, especially if he dies or we divorce

Need own income as then I have greater rights and independence

Sub-ordinates do not accept a woman as boss

Have children, have to look after them and be able to take leave at short notice

Get married, husband doesn't like me working

Not allowed to work night shifts, so miss out on site experience

Have problems being funded at college, have to work part-time

Girls don't study sciences

A challenge - I can do this job

Independent confirmation of abilities - exam results, etc.

Enabling environment - campaigns for more women in engineering

Motivated by social outcome of technical actions

Parental support

Support and attitude of teachers

Colleagues competitive

Need to believe in own abilities

Not taken as seriously

Expectations of male colleagues - can you cope in male dominated environment?

In a minority at university

Maria Ximena Guavita, Ngozi Nora Ishiekwene and Rebecca Scott

The workplace is only one aspect of people's lives. It is worth considering the different roles people may be expected to take on. A female manager may have a high status at work, but domestically, culturally, legally or in religious terms she may have a different status. Similar dislocations can occur with any minority group, when social norms at work conflict with cultural or religious practice outside work. Balancing expectations can be difficult and managers should be aware of the danger of making assumptions and setting programmes that do not consider such issues.

Motivation for action

Action on making an organization more inclusive will have positive and negative impacts on staff and the way they work. One person's freedom to have paternity or maternity leave may be curtailed by another person's need to plan projects. The main issue will be that of power relations. Empowerment of excluded people only moves forward if those with existing authority realise it is in their wider interest to adjust the prevailing distribution of power. Increasing somebody else's status can be perceived as reducing the comparative status of those at the top of the organization. A wider perspective needs to be taken, returning to the reasons for being at work. If a more inclusive workplace motivates staff by enabling them to carry out their work more effectively, the manager should meet the objectives of the organization although personal status may be perceived to have been reduced.

Commitment is needed by all levels of staff within the organization. Awareness raising should relate to people's experiences, so reference to a variety of social groups (based on age, class, caste or religion) may be more appropriate than just concentrating on gender. Policies have to be implemented by people, so all staff should appreciate the issues and be motivated rather than forced to support institutional change.

External monitoring (from funders and clients) and internal reporting can ensure that interest in the issue is maintained. Social change can take a long time and so a mixture of short-term action and long-term planning is required. Any change in an institution will require resources, in staff time, for training and for action. It will also require commitment from senior management.

Practical actions in the office and on site

Throughout these guidelines, methods of ensuring that people often excluded from decision-making are included can be grouped into two categories: short-term, practical measures and longer-term, strategic actions. The same pattern can be seen within an organisation. Practical issues include the physical arrangement of the office and the application of basic work practices.

Physical arrangements

Whether on site or in a permanent office, the physical layout of the working environment can exclude people. The most obvious example is the provision of toilets. Men and women, disabled people and people who prefer to use pedestal or squat-plate toilets all have their specific physical needs. Again, the route to finding a solution is the same as working with the community: consultation and participation in decision-making will enable the assumptions of the decision-makers to be tested.

Other aspects of the work environment can also increase exclusion. Specific issues may be identified by talking to a variety of people in the workforce. Examples include:

- Office layout. Is the office designed to emphasise status or are practical issues given priority? Staff working on drawing boards or CAD computer screens need good lighting conditions. Junior members of the design team working with large drawings need large areas to organise the plans. Secretarial staff are often expected to act also as receptionists and are seated in exposed positions with no privacy. Seating positions within an office can enhance or diminish somebody's authority; are all staff given equal consideration, based on their needs?

- The location of the office itself can discriminate against some people. Travelling to and from work may be different for people who walk, use public transport or have their own transport. Given that women

Site conditions — physical and personal

"Generally when contractors etc are planning their site they neglect to plan for the needs of women – even when I go on site trips now I often have to tell them in advance I'll need size 6 boots ... getting in and out of landrovers etc. However, it is understandable that they don't prepare – how many women can they actually expect to turn up on site? It's catch 22 really."

"Other than that, I would say the preponderance towards aggression is pretty off-putting for some women – they don't generally deal in confrontation so they find it very stressful."

Nina Lovelace, Civil engineering journalist

may have different access to transport, the accessibility of the office can influence their opportunities. If the work is on a building site, would all the workforce benefit from sharing transport? The location of the office or building site may be considered unsafe, especially at night. As women are more likely to have domestic responsibilities as well as their commercial activities, access to shopping and childcare opportunities either on the way to and from the workplace or during lunchtimes may be appreciated.

- When working on site, do men and women have equal access to personal protective equipment, such as boots and safety helmets, where provided?

- Is the office welcoming visually to men and women? Some photographs and calendars can be unacceptable to men or women.

Work practices

The practical management of the staff can limit the type of people who can be employed in the organization and influence their productivity. Men and women have other tasks outside work and these may impact on their ability to work effectively. Domestic activities such as caring for dependants (child and elderly relatives), can be a significant part of the working day. The increase in HIV/AIDS is altering the composition of the traditional family in many parts of the world. Management practices can limit or enhance the effectiveness of all staff. Some examples are given below, but each organization will have its own specific features that need to be identified and addressed.

- Office working hours are often set without consideration of the wider implications. If childcare and shopping has to be fitted around rigid set hours, the domestic arrangements of many staff may be complicated. Flexible hours allow all staff to optimise their own work schedules, including such aspects as avoiding rush-hour traffic or travelling when it is dark. Meetings do not need to be planned at the beginning or end of the working day, or allowed to interrupt meal breaks. Arranging core hours, when all staff are expected to be in, can be a compromise between complete flexibility and the need for people to meet and communicate.

- Does work have to be full-time or can part-time employment be considered?

- Civil engineers are a mobile workforce, especially when working on site. They often work away from the social support network of family and friends. Maternity and paternity leave, leave to return home for funerals and leave for religious festivals can all be regarded as important benefits for staff.

- Staff benefits, such as pay and housing can be allocated in a manner that excludes some staff. In an engineering organization, the main career path will be planned for engineers. Economists, social scientists, environmentalists and administrators may have more barriers to promotion and work benefits. Pay should be determined by equal value to the organisation, not by conforming to a standard career path. Other benefits, such as housing may be allocated according to inappropriate assumptions, such as different conditions for single and married staff.

- Civil engineers often have to travel to work or visit sites. Fieldwork allowances should reflect people's differing circumstances. There may be cultural and practical issues that need to be considered. Can female (or male) staff travel alone safely? Is it acceptable for a woman to travel alone or with male colleagues? Does the extended working day conflict with other responsibilities?

- Are social activities inclusive or exclusive? The timing, location or type of social activity can prevent all staff from taking part. As these activities can be a valuable team-building opportunity, excluding some members of staff for avoidable reasons can reduce the value of the exercise.

- Most workplaces have written or unwritten clothing practices. These can limit the activities of men and women. Long skirts, dresses or saris may not be the most suitable clothes on a building site. Formal clothes in the office can influence the way people act and are treated. This affects both men and women, but social pressure can force people to conform. This can be further complicated by religious practice.

Social actions

Lack of social diversity in the workplace is an issue that has to be addressed socially. Physical and practical actions can reduce barriers and open up opportunities for people normally excluded from positions of power, but if vulnerable people are going to be fully accepted into society, society must change its inequitable practices. Although the actions of individuals and separate organizations may appear to be ineffectual against the prevailing viewpoint, unconnected inclusive actions can contribute to the long-term evolution of society.

Moving people up

A similar process of inclusion can occur in the workplace and on the project. Village water committees often are constituted with a prescribed number of women on them to ensure that their distinctive voice is heard. A similar process can be encouraged within organizations. The presence of women at the higher levels of management can be seen as an indicator of an inclusive organization.

The most direct method is to have women's representatives at various management levels, but this in itself does not cater for other social groups, for example class. It can also isolate women's issues, making them a separate activity from the management of general human resources. Affirmative action can lead to women being given more opportunities for promotion than men, but again this can be perceived as promotion according to quota rather than merit.

A more equitable solution is to examine the reasons why women or people from other excluded groups are not at the highest levels of decision-making. Barriers can be removed and biases allowed for if they can be identified. Many of these procedures will be context specific.

Recruitment

One of the most basic methods of ensuring the workplace has a diverse workforce is to identify recruitment practices that may be restricting opportunities for certain social groups. Some of these may be due to staff only selecting one group or another, for example a male manager may select women because they are less likely to confront his authority or select men as they are supposedly less likely to have childcare issues. The recruitment process has several stages, so advertising, short-listing, interviewing and setting salaries can all bias the procedure towards one social class. A clear specification of the qualities required for the post can provide a benchmark to monitor the recruitment process.

Professional development

In order to progress in a career, through either promotion or changing jobs, men and women need to develop their professional skills. This is carried out through a variety of on the job experience and training and external activities, such as membership of professional groups and individual development courses. If certain members of staff are actively denied opportunities to gain further experience, then their careers can be disrupted. For instance, an unwillingness to provide women with site experience may make it more difficult for them to gain professional qualifications. The bias may be inadvertent, for instance scheduling professional meetings when women have to look after their children or running training courses over a weekend when they have family commitments.

One characteristic that is sometimes quoted is the different work styles of men and women. Whilst this is a generalisation, it has been noted that men often take an adversarial approach (for example when dealing with compensation events and claims on site), whilst women are more likely to negotiate. This lack of overt aggression can be mistaken for passivity rather than an equally (or more) effective method of reaching the same goal. A similar pattern can be observed when it comes to awarding promotions and bonuses, with men more likely to put themselves forward than women.

The tendency for women to work in non-engineering sectors within an engineering organization can also limit opportunities. A specialist is likely to be considered an expert and less suitable for promotion to a management position than an engineer following an already established career path.

Support can also be given through the use of mentors, where individuals are given support outside the line management system, in order to develop their career and address barriers to progress.

Moving power down

In the earlier discussions on participatory project management, we saw how decentralisation brings decision-making nearer to the community. This makes it easier for women and the poor to make their opinions heard. A similar process can be used within an engineering organization. It takes a long time and significant social change for excluded people to reach

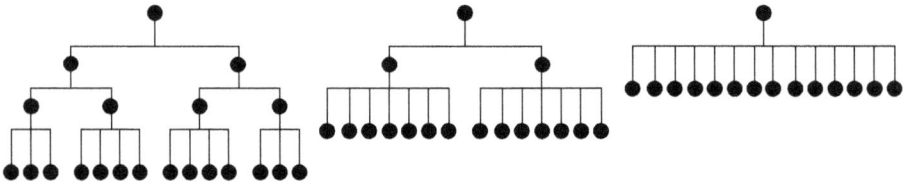

Figure 7.4. Reducing the number of management levels

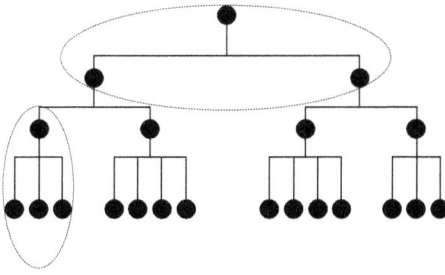

Figure 7.5. Project teams

positions of authority. Within an organization, decision-making can be brought nearer to the bulk of the workforce. There are several options.

If the hierarchy has many levels, these could be reduced to make the pyramidal structure flatter (Figure 7.4).

Flatter organizations are more flexible and adapt more easily to changing circumstances and so are good for project teams designing and building products. The reduction in layers can make communication easier, with both engineering and social benefits. If the structure is too flat however, the communication channels may not be well defined. This may be a problem in stable bureaucracies such as government departments.

If the organization cannot be flattened in terms of management levels, action can be taken within groups, by forming teams working on single projects Figure 7.5). This also promotes communication. Within project teams, unnecessary distinction between levels can be reduced by adopting an inclusive management style rather than trying to lead from the front or manage by decree (Figure 7.6).

If a project approach is used widely within an organization, a hybrid between project teams and a hierarchical approach can be produced (Figure 7.7).

Matrix management allows the multidisciplinary project-team style to work in a more traditional sector management. The structure can be biased, being discipline-led or project-led.

A more decentralised approach involves clustering people together, without any clear distinction in management level (Figure 7.8). This works for dynamic, creative groups.

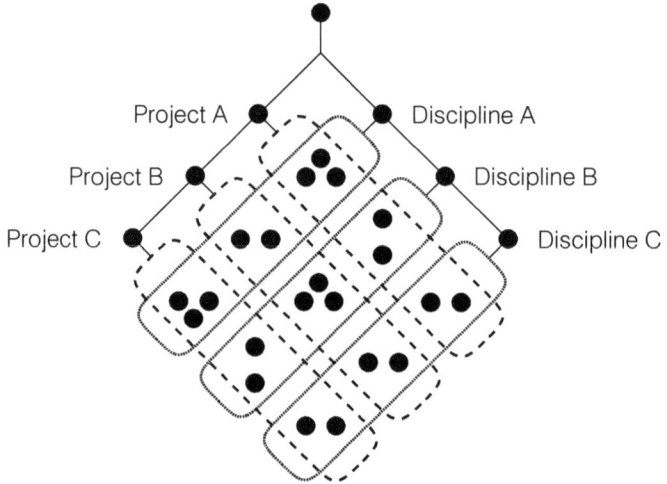

Adapted from Organisational Change Senior B (2002) Financial Times, Prentice Hall UK.

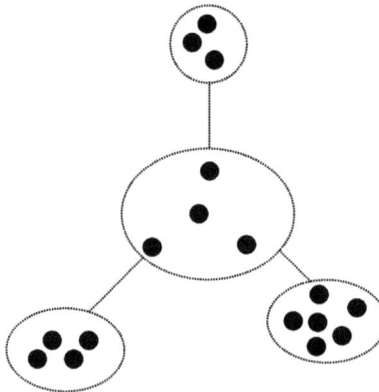

These management structures are practical methods of increasing the involvement in management of the people at the bottom of a hierarchical structure. Reducing the distance (both physical and managerial) between those with decision-making responsibility and those excluded aids participation, consultation and transparency among groups.

Monitoring

Making an organization more inclusive is a process of evolution and institutional learning. The results should be monitored to ensure that progress is being made. The organization will need to carry out internal and external audits of its socio-economic profile at regular intervals to check that the progress and direction are satisfactory.

Conclusions

Engineers have a vital role to play in providing the basic services society needs. The Millennium Development Goals rely on infrastructure to provide economic, social, environmental and physical support to achieve the goals, and they include two directly relevant targets under the Goal of Ensuring Environmental Sustainability:

- Halve, by 2015, the proportion of people without sustainable access to safe drinking water and basic sanitation
- Have achieved, by 2020, a significant improvement in the lives of at least 100 million slum dwellers.

The provision of public services and infrastructure is facing change in the way it operates. Sector reform, decentralisation, privatisation and participation are forcing the change needed to make the provision of infrastructure serve all of society. Engineers are important, as they will not only be providing the technical expertise needed to deliver improved services, but often will be managing projects. Engineers will therefore have to alter what they produce, how they produce it and how they organize themselves. Considering whom they are working for will help direct this change.

The bottom line

Clients, particularly in the private sectors, which have made a mark with innovative procurement and profitable business operations, are consistently those which employ the highest proportion of ethnic minorities and women, which offer staff most opportunity to realise their potential and which reward them for their achievements

New Civil Engineer, 11/04/2002

Checklists

This book covers much of the theory of meeting the needs of men and women using infrastructure services, but the theory has to be put into practice. Each situation is different so a blueprint cannot be expected to work across the whole range of civil engineering projects. However, these checklists have been developed to bring out some of the key points in this book, allowing the reader to revisit the issues at various points of the project process.

These could be used at meetings, for self-assessment at different stages of the project, in preparing designs, plans or reports or as a basis for discussions with project partners and funders.

Project planning

The following notes can be used as a checklist to ensure that issues of social exclusion are integrated into an infrastructure project from the start rather than at a later stage.

Policies

- What are the sector policies and commitments to water coverage (or sanitation or other sector) and social exclusion/gender?
- What are the national policies and commitments to water coverage (or sanitation or other sector) and social exclusion/gender?
- What are the international policies and commitments to water coverage (or sanitation or other sector) and social exclusion/gender?
- Are there social aspects of the water, sanitation or irrigation policies
- Are there practical aspects of gender policies?
- Do the policies work together or conflict? e.g. does cost recovery consider female-headed households?

Goal 1	Eradicate extreme poverty and hunger
Goal 2	Achieve universal primary education
Goal 3	Promote gender equality and empower women
Goal 4	Reduce child mortality
Goal 5	Improve maternal health
Goal 6	Combat HIV/AIDS, malaria, and other diseases
Goal 7	Ensure environmental sustainability
Goal 8	Develop a global partnership for development

Practice

- What approaches are other agencies taking to gender mainstreaming in the sector?

- Does statistical data collection in the sector include appropriate disaggregation by sex, age, tribe, wealth or other relevant indicator of social exclusion?

- Do Terms of Reference require gender issues to be considered in all stages of the project cycle?

Capacity

- Are national and local officials in the sector sufficiently aware of gender issues? If not how can they be encouraged to mainstream gender in their work?

- Does current land, water and credit legislation in practice exclude some members of society from access to services e.g. women, the landless, poor men, and minorities? If so, what measures are in place to alter the 'status quo'?

- Are there economic, social or cultural barriers to women's participation in the planning and implementation of projects? If so, what plans have been made to eliminate these barriers?

- Does the programme strategy include a planned process for building acceptance for gender equality (or other disadvantaged group)? Does this work extend beyond the community level to all operational, support and policy levels to ensure that it takes root?

- Have potential partners been identified in the development of a gender sensitive programme within the local context? Are they involved in the programming process itself?

Strategic issues
- Will the project increase the status and opportunities for women or other disadvantaged groups?

Hints
There are no correct answers to these questions. The local situation will dictate the best way forward. It is important that social exclusion is raised at an early stage, even making it one of the aims of an infrastructure project. Contradictions in policy need to be addressed before the project starts. Look at past programmes and policies to benefit from lessons learnt.

Feasibility study
- What are the rules for selecting projects? Are they clear and have they been agreed?
- Who makes the final decision?
- Who is the 'client'? – The user, the manager or the funder?
- Who are the stakeholders? Do they have representative organizations?
- Have the stakeholders been consulted? – if not, when will they be involved?
- What were they consulted about – were women only asked about social and not technical options?
- Are there any barriers to consultation?
- Do you need somebody acceptable to a group who understands engineering and participation?
- Are any groups constrained from consultations due to time, resources or social restrictions?
- Do all groups have equal information about the project?
- Do all groups have equal opportunities to state their view of the issue and voice their demands?
- Do stakeholder priorities differ?
- Do all groups have equal opportunities to influence decisions?
- Is the project flexible enough to change to meet the needs of users later in the project cycle?
- What are the physical (infrastructure) and social (behaviour) changes necessary to reach the goals?
- What is the physical product of the project (if any)? Can it be used by all people?

- What are the social, economic, environmental impacts of the physical infrastructure?
- Who benefits? – Who pays a cost?
- What are the institutional and management results of the project? Are they open to all people?
- What are the existing power structures? Will they alter?
- What are the social, economic, environmental impacts of the way the project is to be carried out?
- Who benefits? — Who pays a cost?
- Will the project benefit women as well as men, poor as well as rich?
- Is support being provided to enhance the status of socially excluded groups? — both to the group directly and generally in society?
- Are baseline data on current practices and future demands disaggregated by sex wherever possible

Strategic issues
- Will the project increase the status and opportunities for women or other disadvantaged groups?

Hints
There may not be equal opportunities for all and some people will not have complete information, but this state of disparity needs to be recognised and allowed for. Bias may need to be given to disadvantaged groups.

Briefly, re-visit the policy agenda to see if policy is constraining or promoting any aspect of the project at this stage.

Project approval
- What is the project purpose? Does this include a practical and strategic improvement in the position of marginalized people?
- Does the proposed project meet the project purpose?
- Are there any alternatives?
- What are the risks and assumptions? Is one stakeholder group more at risk than other people are?
- What is the long-term sustainability of the project? Who has an interest in keeping it working?
- What are the indicators to be used to measure social aspects of the project? Are these relevant to the core of the project?

Strategic issues

- Is involvement in the project increasing the status and opportunities for women or other disadvantaged groups?

Hints

Review the questions that should have been asked at the previous stages as well. This stage will commit resources (people and money) so it is an opportunity to ensure it proceeds in the correct direction and has the optimum social and physical impact.

Design

Process

- What are the terms of reference/design specification?
- Do the Terms of Reference include social aspects and impacts of engineering?
- Is there going to be participation?
- After consultation, do any of the policies, budgets, programmes and goals need to be revised?
- Who will make the final choice on technology, management system and finance?
- Do all stakeholders accept the participative process – including engineers and funders?
- What indicators are going to be used to measure the involvement of socially excluded groups?

Programme

- Has participation been programmed into the project so there is sufficient time?
- Has it been programmed so information from the community is available before design?
- Has it been programmed so unavailable options are ruled out before being offered?
- Has is been programmed so the community is kept aware of progress and not only consulted when the project team need information?
- Do all stakeholders accept a process approach based on milestones rather than fixed construction schedules – including engineers and funders?

Participation

- Will the participation demonstrate the different (social and physical) needs of the various groups in society?
- Will it encourage dominant groups to accept the need for others' views to be considered?
- Will it encourage the socially excluded groups to contribute?
- Will the community – or sections of the community – require engineering information to make informed choices?
- Will the community – or sections of the community – require economic and management information to make informed choices?
- Does the participation exclude anybody? Think about poor, illiterate women from minority tribal/caste/class groups.
- Can timing, choice of project personnel, type of participation and location increase access?

Preparation

- Is the community involved in collecting engineering data?
- Water sources
- Water use – domestic, commercial and community
- Cropping patterns
- Health data
- Population statistics
- Desired service levels and water consumption of different people
- Existing payment, institutions and management systems
- Ability and willingness to pay – and who will be responsible for capital and operational costs
- Construction practices – how are things built traditionally and who does the work?
- Is all this data separated by sex?

Product

- Are the physical designs suitable for men and women? Have they been asked what they want?
- Is standardisation appropriate in the context of this project? Does the selected technology meet all local demands and preferences?

- Are there any physical, economic or social barriers that prevent men or women from using the infrastructure?
- How are options being communicated to different groups?
- Are different options being offered to individuals, households or neighbourhoods as appropriate? Who makes the choice?
- Does the design suit the construction technique (e.g. poor people may be able to use masonry but concrete would require trained technicians)?

Strategic issues
- Is involvement in the project increasing the status and opportunities for women or other disadvantaged groups?

Hints
The design stage is a significant engineering activity and so you may wish to divide these questions into smaller sections. They may need to be reviewed at various stages of the design.

Construction
- Are men and women willing and able to contribute to the construction of the project?
- Are they to be paid?
- Are there equal opportunities for men and women to participate in paid work (or other rewards)?
- What measure are you going to use for setting payment? Is this fair for men and women?
- How is the division of labour to be allocated?
- Who is going to supervise the work?
- Can women contribute within their daily schedule without becoming overburdened or neglecting other duties (e.g. childcare, subsistence farming, and paid employment)?
- Is there scope for training women as well as men to undertake skilled work?
- Are the proposed construction methods and equipment safe and appropriate for men and women?
- Are the social development opportunities of the construction stage being used?
- Are the people who will be maintaining the systems involved in construction?

- Is the construction programme linked to other activities (e.g. hygiene promotion, management training).
- Can the design be adjusted during construction as people see what is being built?

Strategic issues
- Is involvement in the project increasing the status and opportunities for women or other disadvantaged groups?

Hints
Discussions about the use of tools, construction methods etc. could take place on site.

Payment by piecework may not be fair. Women may be able to dig more of a trench than men can, if men are selected to work on the harder, stony sections.

Different types of work may be paid at different rates. Should people building a roof earn more than the people plastering the walls only because men work on the roof and women work on plastering?

'Voluntary' labour may result in less influential members of society doing all the work.

What are the barriers to women's involvement (lack of skills may require training, illiteracy may mean appropriate contracts have to be used, other responsibilities may necessitate part-time working).

If you are on site, ask people to pick up different sized tools e.g. a lump hammer (300mm long) and a sledgehammer (1000mm long) or a spade and a shovel. Which are more suitable for smaller people?

Operation and maintenance

Management
- Who is responsible for the management of the infrastructure? Are there several layers of management?
- Are men and women represented at each level? Are they active or just making up a quota?
- Are men and women represented in each aspect of the work (e.g. finance and technical)
- Where is the main decision-making power?
- Who are the main users? Are they represented?

Maintenance
- Is the system working?
- Who is employed to carry out maintenance work
- Are there any differences between the work men and women carry out on the system? Do they receive equal reward for equal work?
- Are their any physical, social or economic barriers to women working? Would training, changing the management system, re-assessing the tasks or adapting the infrastructure improve opportunities?

Strategic issues
- Is involvement in the project increasing the status and opportunities for women or other disadvantaged groups?

Hints
This meeting can take place around a water-point or similar focus for the users of a service.

Evaluation

Policy
- What are the policies that formed the project?
- What were the Terms Of Reference?
- What social aspects should have been addressed?

Participation
- Were social issues, such as exclusion of vulnerable groups, included in all aspects (technical, economic, management) rather than just being regarded as a separate issue?
- Were valid stakeholder representatives involved in all stages of the project cycle? What weight was given to contributions from socially excluded groups?
- Were there resources to allow the demands of men and women to be heard and acted upon?
- Who made decisions?
- Did the funders, project staff and other stakeholders not directly using the system accept the involvement of the users?
- Is the evaluation involving all stakeholders?

Practice

- What was the initial assessment of vulnerable groups?
- Were all socially excluded groups recognised (e.g. women included but poor women excluded)?
- Did the design develop to reflect the users' needs?
- Were immediate needs met?
- Is the system working? Can everybody use the system? Is it being used as designed?
- Is there equitable access to the service? – measure number of water points or similar indicators and compare this to social divisions within the community? Do the poor have further to walk?
- How is the system being used? Have patterns of use changed from the initial situation (e.g. men collecting water, women growing commercial crops)?
- Are the users happy with the service? Compare male and female opinions.
- Have people further adapted the service to their needs?

Strategic issues

- Has the project increased the status and opportunities for women or other disadvantaged groups or is it too early to decide?
- Has it made the position worse?
- Are disadvantaged groups more able to take part in managing infrastructure?
- Has the project started other longer-term activities (income generation, social groups)?
- Are the findings of the evaluation going to be shared with the community and other professionals?

Project extension

- Has policy changed since the previous project?
- Have institutions changed since the previous project?
- Has the status of women and the poor changed since the previous project?
- Are all potential users served by the previous project?

Strategic issues

- Will a new project increase the status and opportunities for women or other disadvantaged groups?

A2

Statistical evidence

In a report for the World Bank[64], Deepa Narayan looked at the evidence from 121 rural water supply projects, to see what impact different levels of participation had on the success of each project.

Various factors, such as the quality of implementation, design, construction and operation and maintenance (O&M) as well as levels of participation, were assessed and graded, to see if there were any relationship between the factors and the outcome of the project. The figure below shows that most projects that were graded 'highly effective' also were graded 'high level of participation'.

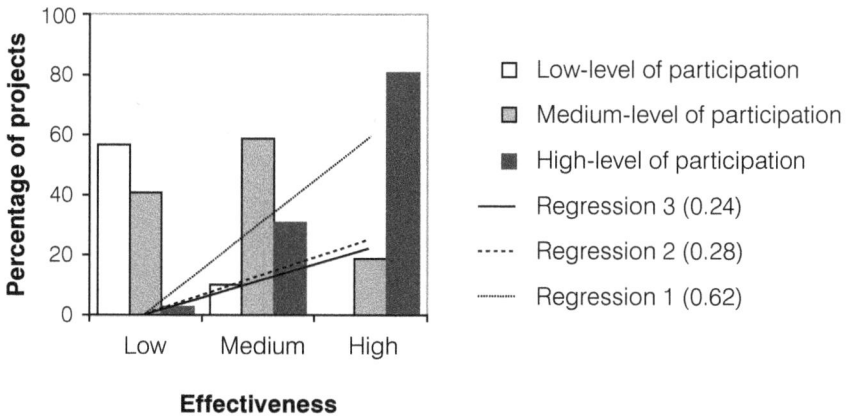

Figure A2.1. Relationship between project effectiveness and level of participation

64. *The Contribution of People's Participation – Evidence from 121 Rural Water Supply Projects*, Deepa Narayan, World Bank, 1995.

In order to assess the significance of the apparent relationship between levels of participation and effectiveness, statistical regressions were used. Three regressions were calculated. The first is a bivariate comparison between effectiveness and participation; this directly compares the two variables, assuming that

$$(effectiveness) = function\ (participation).$$

The second is a multivariate regression including seven other direct factors; the third is multivariate with eleven direct and indirect factors, assuming that

$$(effectiveness) = function\ (participation + implementation$$

$$+\ design + O\&M + etc)$$

This allows for the influence of other variables to be included – for example good management may result in effective projects and participative projects rather than any direct relation between the two factors, i.e.

$$(effectiveness) = function\ (management)$$

and

$$(participation) = function\ (management)$$

but

$$(effectiveness)\ \ function\ (participation)$$

In order to measure the strength of the relationship, statistics can be used to provide a correlation coefficient. A correlation coefficient of 1.0 shows that there is a direct relationship between two factors [i.e. $x=f(y)$]; a coefficient of 0 shows no relationship [i.e. $xf(y)$]; a coefficient between 0 and 1 shows a weaker relationship, but still some connection.

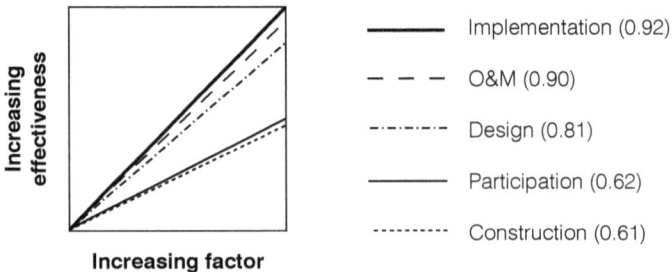

Figure A2.2. Bivariate comparisons between various factors and project effectiveness

Looking at the factors and comparing each with project effectiveness, it can be seen that the most important single factor for project effectiveness is good implementation, followed by good operation and maintenance and good design.

Other relationships between the various factors were also examined. So for example, increasing participation has a strong relationship with strengthening local organizations, but has less impact on local leaders as the participative process can reduce their community role.

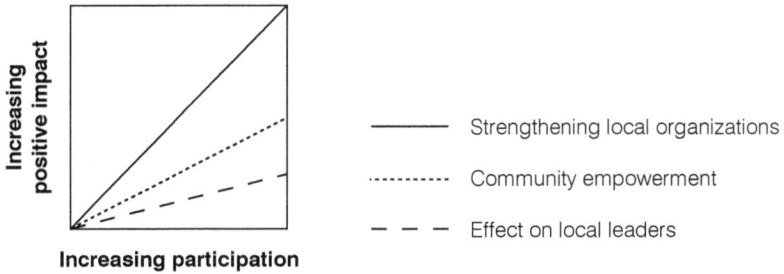

Figure A2.3. Relationships between participation and impact on community organizations

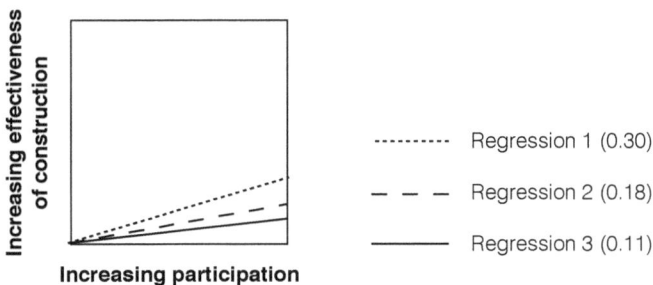

Figure A2.4. Bivariate and multiple regressions — the relationship between effectiveness of construction and participation

The study also looked at the impact participation had on other aspects of the project. The three different regressions show the interconnectedness of the factors in a project. Regression 1 is just between the two factors being looked at (bivariate). Regressions 2 and 3 remove some of the influences that effect both factors (so good management impacts on good construction and participation) and shows a truer picture of the impact of one factor on another.

In theory, more participation should improve design, but the results did not show a strong relationship. Further analysis of the data showed that 'beneficiary participation' did not just include users, but also government staff and other stakeholders with less of a stake in the details of the design. Also only 6 out of the 121 projects examined actually had direct participation in the design of the systems. Other projects used indirect information (market surveys, contingent valuations etc.), which though contributing to the quality of the design, was not considered participative.

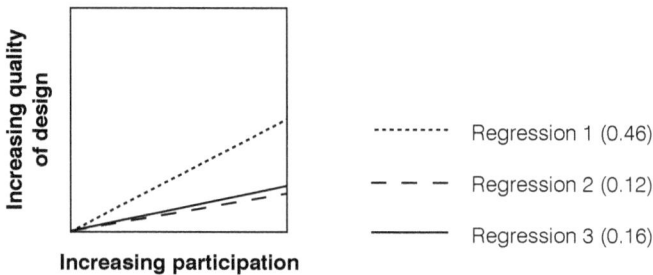

Figure A.2.5. Relationships between participation and impact on design

This illustrates several points:

- that participation in design may be different from participation in a socio-economic sense – a market survey may not be seen as engaging people in depth, but does allow technical information to be gathered from the community
- participation in design was not widespread, even amongst 'participative' projects

- *who* participates is important; each stakeholder has different issues that they are concerned with. Asking an official about pit latrine design may result in concerns about groundwater pollution, whilst asking a women may result in issues about ease of cleaning and fly problems – if the latrine is to be used, the users' concerns are important.

Further reading

- For data on the impact of participation on development projects:
  The Contribution of People's Participation – Evidence from 121 Rural Water Supply Projects
  Deepa Narayan
  World Bank, Washington, USA, 1995

- For information on how to design engineering projects to meet peoples' needs:
  Designing water supply and sanitation projects to meet demand
  Paul Deverill, Simon Bibby, Alison Wedgwood and Ian Smout
  WEDC, Loughborough, UK, 2002

- For information on participative techniques that are gender sensitive:
  Methodology for Participatory Assessments with Communities, Institutions and Policy Makers
  Rekha Dayal, Christine Van Wijk and Nilanjana Mukherjee
  Water and Sanitation Program, March 2000
  or
- *Methodology for Participatory Assessments Training Manual*
  Noma Nyoni and Rose Lidonde
  Water and Sanitation Program, 2002
  and
  Methodology for Participatory Assessments Tool kit
  Noma Nyoni, Rose Lidonde and Mumia Auka
  Water and Sanitation Program, 2002

- For examples of the issues concerning participation by all members of society:

  The Myth of Community – Gender Issues in Participatory Development

  Edited by Irene Guijt and Meera Kaul Shah

  Intermediate Technology Publications, London, UK, 1998

- For information on managing engineering organizations:

  Principles of Engineering Organization

  Stephen Wearne

  Thomas Telford, London UK, 2nd ed., 1993

- For information on how organizations can be managed:

  Management and Organisational Behaviour

  L.J. Mullins

  Prentice Hall, 1999

- For a case study of making NGOs more gender aware organizations

  Macdonald M, Sprenger E and Dubel I. *Gender and Organizational Change: Bridging the Gap Between Policy and Practice* p107 Royal Tropical Institute,

  The Netherlands, 1997

- For training materials to assist engineers in making their workforce more aware of the needs of men and women

  Developing Engineers and Technicians – notes on giving guidance to engineers and technicians on how infrastructure can meet the needs of men and women

  WEDC Loughborough, UK, 2003

- For a review of policies, legal frameworks and institutions from a gender and water perspective, see:

  The Gender and Water Development Report 2003: Gender perspectives on policies in the water sector. Gender and Water Alliance/WEDC, 2003.

- For on-going research and action, see the Gender and Water Alliance Website: http://www.genderandwater.org/